Collins
gem

Greek
phrasebook

Consultant
Maria Koutsoubou

First published 1993
This edition published 2007
Copyright © HarperCollins Publishers
Reprint 10 9 8 7 6 5 4 3 2 1
Typeset by Davidson Pre-Press, Glasgow
Printed in Malaysia by Imago

www.collinslanguage.com

ISBN 13 978-0-00-724670-0

Using your phrasebook

Your *Collins Gem Phrasebook* is designed to help you locate the exact phrase you need, when you need it, whether on holiday or for business. If you want to adapt the phrases, you can easily see where to substitute your own words using the dictionary section, and the clear, full-colour layout gives you direct access to the different topics.

The Gem Phrasebook includes:

- Over 70 topics arranged thematically. Each phrase is accompanied by a simple pronunciation guide which eliminates any problems pronouncing foreign words.

- A Top ten tips section to safeguard against any cultural faux pas, giving essential dos and don'ts for situations involving local customs or etiquette.

- Practical hints to make your stay trouble free, showing you where to go and what to do when dealing with everyday matters such as travel or hotels and offering valuable tourist information.

- Face to face sections so that you understand what is being said to you. These example mini-dialogues give you a good idea of what to expect from a real conversation.

- Common announcements and messages you may hear, ensuring that you never miss the important information you need to know when out and about.

- A clearly laid-out 3000-word dictionary means you will never be stuck for words.

- A basic grammar section which will enable you to build on your phrases.

- A list of public holidays to avoid being caught out by unexpected opening and closing hours, and to make sure you don't miss the celebrations!

It's worth spending time before you embark on your travels just looking through the topics to see what is covered and becoming familiar with what might be said to you.

Whatever the situation, your *Gem Phrasebook* is sure to help!

Contents

Pronouncing Greek

●●●●●●●●●●●●●●●●●●●●●●●●●●●●●●●●●●●●●●

Greek alphabet

Greek is spelt exactly as it sounds. The only difficulty may occur with letters which have the same sound, e.g. υ, η, ι or ει, οι and with double consonants. The names of the 24 letters of the Greek alphabet are given below:

			sound
α, A	άλφα	alfa	ah
β, B	βήτα	veeta	v
γ, Γ	γάμα	ghama	gh
δ, Δ	δέλτα	dhelta	dh
ε, E	έψιλον	epseelon	eh
ζ, Z	ζήτα	zeeta	z
η, H	ήτα	eeta	ee
θ, Θ	θήτα	theeta	th
ι, I	γιώτα	yota	ee
κ, K	κάπα	kapa	k
λ, Λ	λάμδα	lamdha	l
μ, M	μι	mee	m
ν, N	νι	nee	n
ξ, Ξ	ξι	ksee	ks
ο, O	όμικρον	omeekron	oh
π, Π	πι	pee	p

			sound
ρ, Ρ	ρο	ro	r
σ, ς, Σ	σίγμα	seeghma	s
τ, Τ	ταυ	taf	t
υ, Υ	ύψιλον	eepseelon	ee
φ, Φ	φι	fee	f
χ, Χ	χι	khee	kh
ψ, Ψ	ψι	psee	ps
ω, Ω	ωμέγα	omegha	oh

In the pronunciation system used here, Greek sounds are represented by spellings of the nearest possible sounds in English. When you read the pronunciation guide, pronounce the letters as if reading English. The **bold** shows where the stress falls in the word (in the Greek script it is marked with an accent).

	remarks	example	pronunciation
gh	like **r** at back of throat	γάλα	**gh**ala
	where γ is followed by ι or ε, it's	για	(ya)
dh	like **th** in this	δάχτυλο	**dh**akhteelo
th	like **th** in thin	θέατρο	**th**eatro
ks	like **x** in fox	ξένος	ks**e**nos
r	slightly trilled **r**	ρόδα	r**o**dha
kh	like **ch** in loch	χάνω	**kh**ano
	or like a rough **h**	χέρι	kh**e**ree

Here are a few tricky letter combinations:

αι	e	met	γυναίκα	yeen**e**ka
αυ	af	c**af**é	αυτό	aft**o**
	av	or h**av**e	αύριο	**a**vreeo
ει	ee	m**ee**t	είκοσι	**ee**kosee
ευ	ef	**ef**fect	Δευτέρα	dheft**e**ra
	ev	or **ev**ery	Ευρώπη	evr**o**pee
γγ	ng	ha**ng**	Αγγλία	angl**ee**a
γκ	g	**g**et	γκάζι	g**a**zee
	ng	ha**ng**	άγκυρα	**a**ngeera
ντ	nd	ha**nd**	αντίο	and**ee**o
	d	**d**og	ντομάτα	dom**a**ta
μπ	b	**b**ag	μπλούζα	bl**oo**za
οι	ee	m**ee**t	πλοίο	pl**ee**o
ου	oo	m**oo**n	ούζο	**oo**zo

The letters η, ι, υ, οι, and ει have the same sound
ee and αι and ε have the same sound **e** (as in m<u>e</u>t).
You should also note that the Greek question mark
is a semi-colon, i.e. ;.

Top ten tips

••

1 Don't wear beachwear anywhere but at the beach.

2 'Yes' is signified by a slight downward nod of the head; 'no' is a slight upward nod of the head.

3 Nodding your head to indicate 'yes' is not polite; say 'yes' instead.

4 One of the rudest gestures is to thrust the palm of your hand in front of someone's face.

5 It's illegal to play electronic games in cybercafés and in public.

6 Be prepared to be asked about your age, your marital status, etc. Personal questions are commonplace and are not considered rude.

7 Easter is celebrated more than Christmas.

8 Codeine is available on prescription only, so medicines containing codeine should not be brought into Greece.

9 If your passport is stolen, call the tourist police first and they can often act as translators.

10 Names are attached to particular days of the year. For example, if you are called Elena you will celebrate your name day on May 21st. Name day celebrations are as important as birthdays!

Talking to people

Hello/goodbye, yes/no

There are two forms of address in Greek, formal and informal. Greek people use the formal until they are on a first name basis.

Yes	**Ναι**
	ne
No	**Όχι**
	okhee
OK	**Εντάξει**
	end**a**ksee
Please	**Παρακαλώ**
	parakal**o**
Don't mention it	**Παρακαλώ**
	parakal**o**
Excuse me!/sorry!	**Συγνώμη!**
	seeghn**o**mee!
Thank you	**Ευχαριστώ**
	efkhareest**o**

Thanks very much	**Ευχαριστώ πολύ**
	efkhareesto pol**ee**
Sir/Mr	**Κύριε**
	k**ee**ree-e
Madam/Mrs/Ms	**Κυρία**
	keer**ee**a
Miss	**Δεσποινίς**
	dhespeen**ee**s
Hello and	**Γειά σας** (formal)
goodbye	y**a** sas
	Γειά σου (informal)
	y**a** soo
Hello	**Χαίρετε**
	kh**e**rete
Goodbye	**Αντίο**
	and**ee**o
Good morning	**Καλημέρα**
	kaleem**e**ra
Good evening	**Καλησπέρα**
	kaleesp**e**ra
Good night	**Καληνύχτα**
	kaleen**ee**khta
How are you?	**Τι κάνετε;** (formal)
	tee k**a**nete?
	Τι κάνεις; (informal)
	tee k**a**nees?
Very well	**Πολύ καλά**
	pol**ee** kal**a**

14

And you?	**Εσείς;**
	es**ee**s?
I don't	**Δεν καταλαβαίνω**
understand	dhen katalav**e**no
Do you	**Καταλαβαίνετε;**
understand?	katalav**e**nete?
Do you speak	**Μιλάτε αγγλικά;**
English?	meel**a**te angleek**a**?
I speak very little	**Μιλάω πολύ λίγα**
Greek	**ελληνικά**
	meel**a**o pol**ee** l**ee**gha eleeneek**a**

Key phrases

• •

The easiest way to ask for something is by naming
what you want and adding the word for please,
parakalo.

the (masculine)	**o**
	o
(feminine)	**η**
	ee
(neuter)	**το**
	to
the coffee	**ο καφές**
	o kaf**e**s

the beer	**η μπύρα**
	ee b**ee**ra
the glass	**το ποτήρι**
	to pot**ee**ree
a/one coffee	**ένας καφές**
	enas kaf**e**s
a/one beer	**μία μπύρα**
	m**ee**a b**ee**ra
a/one glass	**ένα ποτήρι**
	ena pot**ee**ree
a coffee, please	**έναν καφέ, παρακαλώ**
	enan kaf**e** parakal**o**
a beer, please	**μία μπύρα, παρακαλώ**
	m**ee**a b**ee**ra parakal**o**
a glass of wine, please	**ένα ποτήρι κρασί, παρακαλώ**
	ena pot**ee**ree kras**ee** parakal**o**
my passport	**το διαβατήριό μου**
	to dheeavat**ee**ree**o** moo
my room	**το δωμάτιό μου**
	to dhom**a**tee**o** moo
I'd like...	**Θα ήθελα...**
	tha **ee**thela...
I'd like an ice cream	**Θα ήθελα ένα παγωτό**
	tha **ee**thela **e**na paghot**o**
We'd like...	**Θα θέλαμε...**
	tha th**e**lame...
We'd like two rooms	**Θα θέλαμε δύο δωμάτια**
	tha th**e**lame dh**ee**o dhom**a**teea

We'd like to go to Athens	**Θα θέλαμε να πάμε στην Αθήνα**
	tha th**e**lame na p**a**me steen ath**ee**na
Do you have...?	**Έχετε...;**
	ekhete...?
Do you have bread?	**Έχετε ψωμί;**
	ekhete psom**ee**?
Do you have milk?	**Έχετε γάλα;**
	ekhete gh**a**la?
How much is it?	**Πόσο κάνει;**
	p**o**so k**a**nee?
How much does ... cost?	**Πόσο κοστίζει ο/η/το...;**
	p**o**so kost**ee**zee o/ee/to...?
How much is the wine?	**Πόσο κάνει το κρασί;**
	poso k**a**nee to kras**ee**?
How much does the ticket cost?	**Πόσο κοστίζει το εισιτήριο;**
	p**o**so kost**ee**zee to eeseet**ee**reeo?
large	**μεγάλο**
	megh**a**lo
small	**μικρό**
	meekr**o**
with	**με**
	me
without	**χωρίς**
	khor**ee**s
Where is...?	**Πού είναι...;**
	poo **ee**ne...?

Where is the toilet?	**Πού είναι η τουαλέτα;**
	poo **ee**ne ee tooal**e**ta?
Where is the nearest bank?	**Πού είναι η κοντινότερη τράπεζα;**
	poo **ee**ne ee kondeen**o**teree tr**a**peza?
When does it open?	**Πότε ανοίγει;**
	p**o**te an**ee**yee?
When does it close?	**Πότε κλείνει;**
	pote kl**ee**nee?
today	**σήμερα**
	s**ee**mera
tonight	**απόψε**
	ap**o**pse
tomorrow	**αύριο**
	avreeo
yesterday	**χθες**
	khthes
Can I...?	**Μπορώ να...;**
	bor**o** na...?
Can I pay?	**Μπορώ να πληρώσω;**
	bor**o** na pleer**o**so?

Signs and notices

ΑΝΟΙΚΤΟ	open
ΚΛΕΙΣΤΟ	closed
ΣΕΛΦ ΣΕΡΒΙΣ	self-service
ΕΙΣΟΔΟΣ	entrance
ΕΞΟΔΟΣ	exit
ΤΑΜΕΙΟ	cash desk
ΩΘΗΣΑΤΕ	push
ΣΥΡΑΤΕ	pull
ΤΟΥΑΛΕΤΕΣ	toilets
ΚΕΝΤΡΟ	centre
ΑΝΔΡΩΝ	gents
ΓΥΝΑΙΚΩΝ	ladies
ΔΕΝ ΛΕΙΤΟΥΡΓΕΙ	out of order
ΚΑΤΕΙΛΗΜΜΕΝΟ	engaged
ΠΛΗΡΟΦΟΡΙΕΣ	information
ΕΝΟΙΚΙΑΖΕΤΑΙ	for hire/to rent
ΠΩΛΕΙΤΑΙ	for sale
ΕΚΠΤΩΣΕΙΣ	sales
ΔΩΜΑΤΙΑ	rooms
ΜΟΥΣΕΙΟ	museum
ΙΔΙΩΤΙΚΟΣ ΧΩΡΟΣ	private
ΗΜΕΡΟΜΗΝΙΑ	date
ΜΗΝ ΑΓΓΙΖΕΤΕ	do not touch
ΑΠΑΓΟΡΕΥΕΤΑΙ ΤΟ ΜΠΑΝΙΟ	no bathing

ΑΠΑΓΟΡΕΥΕΤΑΙ Η ΕΙΣΟΔΟΣ	no entry
ΚΑΠΝΙΖΟΝΤΕΣ	smoking
ΑΠΑΓΟΡΕΥΕΤΑΙ ΤΟ ΚΑΠΝΙΣΜΑ	no smoking
ΑΠΑΓΟΡΕΥΕΤΑΙ Η ΣΤΑΘΜΕΥΣΗ	no parking
ΑΠΑΓΟΡΕΥΕΤΑΙ Η ΚΑΤΑΣΚΗΝΩΣΗ	no camping
ΑΠΑΓΟΡΕΥΕΤΑΙ Η ΕΙΣΟΔΟΣ	no entry
ΙΣΟΓΕΙΟ	ground floor
ΕΙΣΙΤΗΡΙΑ	tickets
ΕΟΤ	Greek Tourist Office
ΦΥΛΑΞΗ ΑΠΟΣΚΕΥΩΝ	left luggage

I have ... children	Έχω ... παιδιά
	ekho ... pedhy**a**
I have no children	Δεν έχω παιδιά
	dhen **e**kho pedhy**a**
I'm here...	Βρίσκομαι εδώ...
	vr**ee**skome edh**o**...
on holiday	για διακοπές
	ya dheeakop**es**
for work	για δουλειά
	ya dhooly**a**

Work

What work do you do?	Τι δουλειά κάνετε;
	tee dhooly**a** k**a**nete?
Do you enjoy it?	Σας αρέσει;
	sas ar**e**see?
I'm...	Είμαι...
	eeme...
a doctor	γιατρός
	yatr**os**
a teacher (male/female)	δάσκαλος/δασκάλα
	dh**a**skalos/dhask**a**la
I'm self-employed	Έχω δουλειά δική μου
	eho dhooly**a** dheek**ee** moo

25

Weather

It's sunny **Έχει ήλιο**
ekhee eelyo

It's very hot **Κάνει πολύ ζέστη**
kanee polee zestee

It's windy **Έχει αέρα**
ekhee aera

What awful **Τι απαίσιος καιρός!**
weather! tee apeseeos keros!

What will the **Τι καιρό θα κάνει αύριο;**
weather be tee kero tha kanee avreeo?
like tomorrow?

What is the **Τι θερμοκρασία έχει;**
temperature? tee thermokraseea ekhee?

Getting around

Asking the way

απέναντι apenantee		opposite
δίπλα στο/στην dheepla sto/steen		next to
κοντά στο/στην konda sto/steen		near to
φανάρια fanarya		traffic lights
στη γωνία stee ghoneea		at the corner
στην πλατεία steen plateea		in the square

I'm looking for...	**ψάχνω για…** psakhno ya...
Can I walk there?	**Μπορώ να πάω με τα πόδια;** boro na pao me ta podhya?
We're lost	**Έχουμε χαθεί** ekhoome khathee
Is this the way to...?	**Πάω καλά για…;** pao kala ya...?

27

A Με συγχωρείτε! Πώς θα πάω στο σταθμό;
me seenkhor**ee**te! p**o**s tha p**a**o sto stathm**o**?
Excuse me, how do I get to the station?

B Όλο ευθεία και μετά την εκκλησία στρίψτε
αριστερά/δεξιά!
olo efth**ee**a ke met**a** teen eklees**ee**a str**i**pste
areester**a**/dheks**ee**a!
Keep straight on, after the church turn left/right!

A Είναι μακρυά;
eene makree**a**?
Is it far?

B Όχι, περίπου 400 μ/πέντε λεπτά
okhi, per**ee**pou 400 m./p**e**nte lept**a**
No, 4 metres/five minutes

A Ευχαριστώ!
efkharist**o**!
Thank you!

B Παρακαλώ
parakal**o**
You're welcome

Is it far?	**Είναι μακριά;**
	eene makree**a**?
How do I get onto the motorway?	**Πώς θα βγω στην εθνική οδό;**
	p**o**s tha vgho steen ethneek**ee** odh**o**?
Can you show me where it is on the map?	**Μπορείτε να μου το δείξετε πάνω στο χάρτη;**
	bor**ee**te na moo to dh**ee**ksete p**a**no sto kh**a**rtee?

YOU MAY HEAR...

Στρίψτε δεξιά/ αριστερά str**ee**pste dheksee**a**/areester**a**	Turn right/left
Προχωρήστε ευθεία μέχρι να φτάσετε... prokhor**ee**ste efth**ee**a m**e**khree na ft**a**sete...	Keep straight on until you get...
στη διασταύρωση stee dheeast**a**vrosee	to the junction

> **Maps and guides** (p 69)

Bus and coach

....

Bus is the major form of overland transport in
Greece and Cyprus and there is a good network of
local and long-distance routes. On some routes you
must buy a ticket before you depart.

FACE TO FACE

A Συγνώμη, ποιό λεωφορείο πάει στο
κέντρο;
seeghn**o**mee, py**o** lefor**ee**o p**a**ee sto k**e**ntro?
Excuse me, which bus goes to the centre?

B Το νούμερο 15
to n**oo**mero 15
Number 15

A Πού είναι η στάση;
poo **ee**ne ee st**a**see?
Where is the bus stop?

B Εκεί δεξιά
ek**ee** dheks**ee**a
There, on the right

A Πού μπορώ να αγοράσω εισιτήρια;
poo bor**o** na aghor**a**so eeseet**ee**reea?
Where can I buy tickets?

B Στο περίπτερο
sto per**ee**ptero
At the kiosk

30

Is there a bus to...?	**Υπάρχει λεωφορείο για...;** eep**a**rkhee leofor**ee**o ya...?
Where do I catch the bus to...?	**Από πού θα πάρω το λεωφορείο για...;** ap**o** poo tha p**a**ro to leofor**ee**o ya...?
We're going to...	**Πηγαίνουμε στο...** peey**e**noome sto...
How much is it...?	**Πόσο κάνει...;** p**o**so k**a**nee...?
to the beach	**για τη θάλασσα** ya tee th**a**lasa
to the airport	**για το αεροδρόμιο** ya to aerodhr**o**meeo
How often are the buses to...?	**Κάθε πότε έχει λεωφορείο για...;** k**a**the p**o**te **e**khee leofor**ee**o ya...?
When is	**Πότε είναι** p**o**te **ee**ne
the first	**το πρώτο** to pr**o**to
the last	**το τελευταίο** to teleft**e**o
bus	**λεωφορείο** leofor**ee**o
to...?	**για...;** ya ...?

Please can you tell me when to get off?	**Παρακαλώ, μπορείτε να μου πείτε πότε να κατέβω;**
	parakalo boreete na moo peete pote na katevo?
This is my stop	**Αυτή είναι η στάση μου**
	aftee eene ee stasee moo

YOU MAY HEAR...

Το λεωφορείο αυτό δε σταματά στο...	This bus doesn't stop in...
to leoforeeo afto dhe stamata sto...	
Πρέπει να πάρετε το...	You have to catch the...
prepee na parete to...	

Metro

The new metro system in Athens opens at 5.30 am and closes at midnight. A ticket is valid for one single journey of any length. You can also get a 24-hour ticket. There are armed police on patrol at stations. It is forbidden to eat or drink in the stations and on the metro.

| Where is the metro station? | **Πού είναι ο σταθμός του μετρό;** |
| | poo eene o stathmos too metro? |

(for old electric line)	**του ηλεκτρικού;**
	too eelektreek**oo**?
A ticket	**Ένα εισιτήριο**
	ena eeseet**ee**reeo
A 24-hour ticket	**Ένα ημερήσιο εισιτήριο**
	ena eemer**ee**seeo eeseet**ee**reeo
4 tickets, please	**Τέσσερα εισιτήρια**
	παρακαλώ
	t**e**sera eeseet**ee**reea parakal**o**
Do you have an underground map?	**Έχετε ένα χάρτη με τις**
	γραμμές του μετρό;
	ekhete **e**na kh**a**rtee me tees
	ghramm**e**s too metr**o**?
I want to go to...	**Θέλω να πάω στο/στη...**
	th**e**lo na p**a**o sto/stee...
Do I have to change?	**Πρέπει να αλλάξω τρένο;**
	pr**e**pee na al**a**kso tr**e**no?
Where?	**Πού;**
	poo?
Which line do I take?	**Ποια γραμμή πρέπει να**
	πάρω;
	pya ghramm**ee** pr**e**pee na p**a**ro?

Train

· ·

Train services in Greece are limited and slow by
comparison with other western European railways.
There is only one main line, operated by Greek
Railways **ΟΣΕ**, running from Athens north to
Thessaloniki and onwards to Bulgaria, Turkey and
the former Yugoslavia. The Peloponnese is served
by a narrow-gauge line from Athens. There are no
trains on Cyprus.

FACE TO FACE

A **Πότε είναι το τρένο για...;**
pote **ee**ne to tr**e**no ya...?
When is the train to...?

B **Στις πέντε και δέκα**
stees p**e**nte ke dh**e**ka
At ten past five

A **Θα ήθελα δύο εισιτήρια παρακαλώ**
tha **ee**thela dh**ee**o eeseet**ee**reea parakal**o**
I'd like two tickets, please

B **απλό εισιτήριο ή με επιστροφή;**
apl**o** eeseet**ee**reeo **ee** me epeestrof**ee**?
Single or return?

| Where is the train station? | **Πού είναι ο σταθμός τρένου;** |
| | poo **ee**ne o stathm**os** tr**e**noo? |

34

To the station, please	**Στο σταθμό παρακαλώ**	sto stathm**o** parakal**o**
A single to...	**Ένα απλό εισιτήριο για…**	**e**na apl**o** eeseet**ee**reeo ya…
Two singles to...	**Δύο απλά εισιτήρια για…**	dh**ee**o apl**a** eeseet**ee**reea ya…
A return to...	**Ένα εισιτήριο με επιστροφή για…**	**e**na eeseet**ee**reeo me epeestrof**ee** ya…
Two return tickets to...	**Δύο εισιτήρια με επιστροφή για…**	dh**ee**o eeseet**ee**reea me epeestrof**ee** ya…
Economy class	**Τουριστική θέση**	tooreesteek**ee** thesee
Smoking	**Καπνίζοντες**	kapn**ee**zontes
Non smoking	**Μη καπνίζοντες**	mee kapn**ee**zontes
I want to book a seat to Thessaloniki	**Θέλω να κλείσω ένα εισιτήριο για τη Θεσσαλονίκη**	th**e**lo na kl**ee**so **e**na eeseet**ee**reeo ya tee thesalon**ee**kee
When does it arrive in...?	**Πότε φτάνει στο…;**	p**o**te ft**a**nee sto…?
Do I have to change?	**Πρέπει να αλλάξω;**	pr**e**pee na al**a**kso?

Train

35

Where?	**Πού;**
	poo?
Which platform does it leave from?	**Από ποια πλατφόρμα φεύγει;**
	apo pya platforma fevyee?
Is this the train for...?	**Αυτό είναι το τρένο για…;**
	afto eene to treno ya...?
When will it leave?	**Πότε θα φύγει;**
	pote tha feeyee?
Why is the train delayed?	**Γιατί έχει καθυστέρηση το τρένο;**
	yatee ekhee katheestereesee to treno?
Does the train stop at...?	**Σταματάει το τρένο στο…;**
	stamataee to treno sto...?
Please let me know when we get to...	**Μου λέτε, σας παρακαλώ, πότε φτάνουμε στο…**
	moo lete, sas parakalo, pote ftanoome sto...
Is this free? (seat)	**Είναι ελεύθερη;**
	eene eleftheree?
Excuse me	**Με συγχωρείτε**
	me seenkhoreete

> **Luggage** (p 90)

Taxi

....

If you plan to take a taxi from the airport, check with the information desk how much the fare should be.

I need a taxi	**Χρειάζομαι ταξί** khree**a**zome taks**ee**
Where can I get a taxi?	**Πού μπορώ να πάρω ένα ταξί;** poo bor**o** na p**a**ro **e**na taks**ee**?
How much is a taxi...?	**Πόσο κάνει το ταξί...;** p**o**so k**a**nee to taks**ee**...?
to the station	**για το σταθμό** ya to stathm**o**
to the airport	**για το αεροδρόμιο** ya to aerodhr**o**meeo
to the centre	**για το κέντρο** ya to k**e**ntro
Please take me (us) to...	**Παρακαλώ πηγαίνετέ με (μας) στο...** parakal**o** peey**e**net**e** me (mas) sto...
Why are you charging me so much?	**Γιατί με χρεώνετε τόσο πολύ;** yat**ee** me khre**o**nete t**o**so pol**ee**?
Keep the change	**Κρατήστε τα ρέστα** krat**ee**ste ta r**e**sta

37

Sorry, I don't	Συγνώμη, δεν έχω ψιλά
have change	seeghn**o**mee, dhen **e**kho pse**e**la
I have to catch...	Πρέπει να προλάβω...
	pr**e**pee na prol**a**vo...
the ... o'clock	την πτήση των ... για το...
flight to...	teen pt**ee**see ton ... ya to...

Boat and ferry

● ●

In Greece, with its many islands, ferries are an
important means of transport. The centre of the
ferry network is the port of Piraeus. Hydrofoils –
ιπτάμενο δελφίνι (eept**a**meno dhelf**ee**nee) 'flying
dolphins' – operate between Piraeus and the nearer
islands.

When is the next	Πότε φεύγει το επόμενο
boat to...?	πλοίο για...;
	p**o**te f**e**vyee to ep**o**meno
	pl**ee**o ya...?
Have you	Έχετε ωρολόγιο
a timetable?	πρόγραμμα;
	ekhete orol**o**yeeo pr**o**ghrama?
Is there a boat	Υπάρχει πλοίο για...;
to...?	eep**a**rkhee pl**ee**o ya...?
How much is	Πόσο κάνει ένα εισιτήριο...;
a ticket...?	p**o**so k**a**nee **e**na eeseet**ee**reeo...?

single	**απλό**
	apl**o**
return	**με επιστροφή**
	me epeestrof**ee**
How long is the journey?	**Πόσο διαρκεί το ταξίδι;**
	p**o**so dheeark**ee** to taks**ee**dhee?
What time do we get to...?	**Τι ώρα φτάνουμε στο...;**
	tee **o**ra ft**a**noome sto...?
Where does the boat leave from?	**Από πού φεύγει το πλοίο;**
	ap**o** poo f**e**vyee to pl**ee**o?
When is...?	**Πότε είναι...;**
	p**o**te **ee**ne...?
the first...	**το πρώτο...**
	to pr**o**to...
the last...	**το τελευταίο...**
	to teleft**e**o...
hydrofoil	**ιπτάμενο δελφίνι**
	eept**a**meno dhelf**ee**nee
boat	**πλοίο**
	pl**ee**o
ferry	**φεριμπότ**
	fereeb**ot**

Air travel

Most signs are in Greek and English and you may go through the airport without having to speak any Greek. If you are arriving at Athens on a non-Greek carrier and have a domestic flight to catch, allow plenty of time to get across the airport. Greece is highly security-conscious and it is against the law to take photographs of airports.

ΑΦΙΞΕΙΣ afeeksees	arrivals
ΕΙΣΟΔΟΣ eesodhos	entrance
ΕΞΟΔΟΣ eksodhos	exit
ΑΝΑΧΩΡΗΣΕΙΣ anakhoreesees	departures
ΠΤΗΣΗ pteesee	flight

To the airport, please	**Στο αεροδρόμιο, παρακαλώ** sto aerodhromeeo, parakalo
How do I get to the airport?	**Πώς μπορώ να πάω στο αεροδρόμιο;** pos boro na pao sto aerodhromeeo
Is there a bus to the city centre?	**Υπάρχει λεωφορείο για το κέντρο της πόλης;** eeparkhee leoforeeo ya to kendro tees polees?

Where do I check in for...(airline)?	**Πού γίνεται ο έλεγχος αποσκευών για...;**
	poo y**ee**nete o **e**lenhos aposkev**o**n ya...?
Which gate is it for the flight to...?	**Ποια είναι η έξοδος της πτήσης για...;**
	pya **ee**ne ee **e**ksodhos tees pt**ee**sees ya...?

Air travel

> **Luggage** (p 90) > **Taxi** (p 37)

Customs control

You will not be allowed to enter Greece or Cyprus if your passport has a stamp from the Turkish Republic of Northern Cyprus. You will need an export permit if you plan to take home any antiquities, including old icons, even if they appear to have little or no archaeological or commercial value. Both the Greek and Cypriot authorities are very sensitive about the illegal export of antiquities, so should you be caught do not expect clemency. With the single European market, passengers arriving from a member state of the European Union are subject only to highly selective spot checks and they can go through the blue customs channel.

Do I have to pay duty on this?	**Πρέπει να πληρώσω φόρο γι' αυτό;**
	prepee na pleeroso foro yafto?
It is for my own personal use	**Είναι για προσωπική μου χρήση**
	eene ya prosopeekee moo khreesee
We are on our way to...	**Πηγαίνουμε για...**
	peegenoome ya...

42

Driving

Car hire

....

το δίπλωμα οδήχηεης	driving licence
to dh**ee**ploma odh**ee**yeesees	
η οπίσθεν ee **o**peesthen	reverse gear

I want to hire a car	**Θέλω να νοικιάσω ένα αυτοκίνητο**
	th**e**lo na neeky**a**so **e**na aftok**ee**neeto
for ... days	**για ... μέρες**
	ya ... m**e**res
How much is it...?	**Πόσο κάνει...;**
	p**o**so k**a**nee...?
per day	**τη μέρα**
	tee m**e**ra
per week	**τη βδομάδα**
	tee vdhom**a**dha
How much is the deposit?	**Πόση είναι η προκαταβολή;**
	p**o**see **ee**ne ee prokatavol**ee**?

43

Is there a charge per kilometre?	**Γίνεται χρέωση ανά χιλιόμετρο;** y**ee**nete khr**e**osee an**a** kheely**o**metro?
What is included in the insurance?	**Τι περιλαμβάνεται στην ασφάλεια;** tee pereelamv**a**nete steen asf**a**leea?
Do I have to return the car here?	**Πρέπει να γυρίσω το αυτοκίνητο εδώ;** pr**e**pee na yeer**ee**so to aftok**ee**neeto edh**o**?
What time?	**Τι ώρα;** tee **o**ra?
I'd like to leave it in...	**Θα ήθελα να το αφήσω στο...** tha **ee**thela na to af**ee**so sto...
What do I do if I break down?	**Τι θα κάνω αν μείνω από βλάβη;** tee tha k**a**no an m**ee**no ap**o** vl**a**vee?

YOU MAY HEAR...

Μπορείτε να γυρίσετε το αυτοκίνητο με άδειο ρεζερβουάρ bor**ee**te na yeer**ee**sete to aftok**ee**neeto me **a**dheeo rezervoo**ar**	You can return the car with an empty tank

44

Motorbike hire

. . . .

Hiring a motorbike is a popular and economical form of transport in both Greece and Cyprus. Motorbikes are however the cause of a great number of injuries. Regulations requiring the wearing of crash helmets are widely flouted. When hiring, check that the machine is mechanically sound and that insurance is provided.

I want to hire...	**Θέλω να νοικιάσω…**
	th**e**lo na neeky**a**so...
a motorcycle	**μοτοσυκλέτα**
	motoseekl**e**ta
a moped	**μοτοποδήλατο**
	motopodh**ee**lato
for a day	**για μία μέρα**
	ya m**ee**a m**e**ra
for the morning	**για το πρωί**
	ya to pro**ee**
for the afternoon	**για το απόγευμα**
	ya to ap**o**yevma
Is a crash helmet included in the price?	**Το κράνος περιλαμβάνεται στην τιμή;**
	to kr**a**nos pereelamv**a**nete steen teem**ee**?

Is insurance included in the price?	**Η ασφάλιση περιλαμβάνεται στην τιμή;** ee asfaleesee pereelamvanete steen teemee?
I want to pay by credit card	**Θέλω να πληρώσω με πιστωτική κάρτα** thelo na pleeroso me peestoteekee karta
What is your phone number?	**Ποιος είναι ο αριθμός του τηλεφώνου σας;** pyos eene o areethmos too teelefonoo sas?

Driving

Try to avoid driving in the major cities, particularly Athens. Traffic congestion can be appalling and parking in city centres almost impossible. Drive on the right in Greece but on the left in Cyprus.

Can I park here?	Μπορώ να παρκάρω εδώ; boro na parkaro edho?
How long for?	Για πόση ώρα; ya posee ora?
Where can I park?	Πού μπορώ να παρκάρω; poo boro na parkaro?
Do I need a parking ticket?	Χρειάζομαι κάρτα στάθμευσης; khreeazome karta stathmefsees?
We're going to...	Πηγαίνουμε στο... peeyenoome sto...
Which junction is it for...?	Σε ποια διασταύρωση είναι...; se pya dheeastavrosee eene...?

Petrol

ΑΜΟΛΥΒΔΗ amoleevdhee	unleaded
ΠΕΤΡΕΛΑΙΟ petreleo	diesel
ΒΕΝΖΙΝΗ venzeenee	petrol

Is there a petrol station near here?
Υπάρχει βενζινάδικο εδώ κοντά;
eep**a**rkhee venzeen**a**dheeko edh**o** kond**a**?

Fill it up, please
Γεμίστε το, παρακαλώ
yem**ee**ste to parakal**o**

Please check the oil/the water
Παρακαλώ ελέγξτε τα λάδια/το νερό
parakal**o** el**e**nkste ta l**a**dhya/ to ner**o**

20 euros worth of unleaded petrol
Είκοσι ευρώ αμόλυβδη βενζίνη
eekosee evr**o** am**o**leevdhee venz**ee**nee

Where is...?
Πού είναι...;
poo **ee**ne...?

the air line
η παροχή του αέρα
ee parokh**ee** too a**e**ra

the water
το νερό
to ner**o**

Driving

48

Please check the tyres	**Παρακαλώ ελέγξτε τα λάστιχα**
	parakalo elenkste ta lasteekha
Can I pay with this credit card?	**Μπορώ να πληρώσω με αυτή την κάρτα;**
	boro na pleeroso me aftee tee karta?

Breakdown

Can you help me?	**Μπορείτε να με βοηθήσετε;**
	boreete na me voeetheesete?
My car has broken down	**Το αυτοκίνητό μου χάλασε**
	to aftokeeneeto moo khalase
Is there a garage near here?	**Υπάρχει συνεργείο εδώ κοντά;**
	eeparkhee seeneryeeo edho konda?
The car won't start	**Το αυτοκίνητο δεν ξεκινά**
	to aftokeeneeto dhen ksekeena
Can you give me a push?	**Μπορείτε να σπρώξετε;**
	boreete na sproksete?
I've run out of petrol	**Έμεινα από βενζίνη**
	emeena apo venzeenee

Can you tow me to the nearest garage?	Μπορείτε να με τραβήξετε μέχρι το κοντινότερο συνεργείο;
	bor**ee**te na me trav**ee**ksete m**e**khree to kondeen**o**tero seenery**ee**o?

Car parts

. . . .

The ... doesn't work	ο/η/το ... δε λειτουργεί
	o/ee/to ... dhe leetooryee
The ... don't work	οι/τα ... δε λειτουργούν
	ee/ta ... dhe leetoorgh**oo**n

accelerator	το γκάζι	g**a**zee
battery	η μπαταρία	batar**ee**a
brakes	τα φρένα	fr**e**na
choke	το τσοκ	tsok
clutch	ο συμπλέκτης	seembl**e**ktees
engine	η μηχανή	meekhan**ee**
exhaust pipe	η εξάτμιση	eks**a**tmeesee
fuse	η ασφάλεια	asf**a**leea
gears	οι ταχύτητες	takh**ee**teetes
handbrake	το χειρόφρενο	kheer**o**freno
headlights	τα φώτα	ta f**o**ta
ignition	η ανάφλεξη	an**a**fleksee
indicator	το φλας	flas

radiator	το ψυγείο	pseeyeeo
rear lights	τα πίσω φώτα	peeso fota
seat belt	η ζώνη ασφαλείας	zonee asfaleeas
spare wheel	η ρεζέρβα	rezerva
spark plug	το μπουζί	boozee
steering wheel	το τιμόνι	teemonee
tyre	το λάστιχο	lasteekho
wheel	η ρόδα	rodha
windscreen	το παρμπρίζ	parbreez
wiper	ο υαλοκαθ-αριστήρας	eealokatharee-steeras

Road signs

camping

customs control

restricted parking
zone

end to restricted
parking zone

directional sign

north

βορράς

west δύση ανατολή east

νότος

south

no parking in
odd-numbered
months

no parking in
even-numbered
months

motorway toll

parking for
card holders

Speed limits in Greece
are in kilometres

parking for taxis

Staying somewhere

Hotel (booking)

It is best to book accommodation in advance, particularly in the more popular resorts in high season. If you do get stuck for a place to stay, a branch of the Greek Tourist Organisation (or Cyprus Tourism Organisation in Cyprus) may be able to help.

FACE TO FACE

A **Θα ήθελα ένα δίκλινο/μονόκλινο δωμάτιο**
tha **ee**thela **e**na dh**ee**kleeno/mon**o**kleeno dhom**a**teeo
I'd like a double/single room

B **Για πόσες νύχτες;**
ya p**o**ses n**ee**khtes?
For how many nights?

A **Για μια νύχτα/... νύχτες**
ya mya n**ee**khta/... n**ee**khtes
for one night/... nights

ΞΕΝΟΔΟΧΕΙΟ ksenodhokh**ee**o	hotel	
ΔΩΜΑΤΙΑ dhom**a**teea	rooms (often in private houses)	

Do you have any vacancies?	**Έχετε ελεύθερα δωμάτια;** **e**khete el**e**fthera dhom**a**teea?
for tonight	**για απόψε;** ya ap**o**pse?
We'd like to stay ... nights	**Θα θέλαμε να μείνουμε ... βράδυα** tha th**e**lame na m**ee**noome ... vr**a**dheea
from ... till...	**από ... μέχρι...** ap**o** ... m**e**khree...
How much is it per day/ per week?	**Πόσο κοστίζει για μια μέρα/μια βδομάδα;** p**o**so kost**ee**zee ya mya m**e**ra/ mya vdom**a**da?
for three people	**τρίκλινο** tr**ee**kleeno
with bath	**με μπάνιο** me b**a**nyo
with shower	**με ντους** me doos
with a double bed	**με διπλό κρεβάτι** me dheepl**o** krev**a**tee
twin-bedded	**με δύο κρεβάτια** me dh**ee**o krev**a**tya

55

A room looking onto the sea	Ένα δωμάτιο που να βλέπει στη θάλασσα
	ena dhomateeo poo na vlepee stee thalasa
How much is it...?	Πόσο κοστίζει...;
	poso kosteezee...?
per night	το βράδυ
	to vradhee
per week	τη βδομάδα
	tee vdhomadha
for half board	με ημιδιατροφή
	me eemeedheeatrofee
for full board	με πλήρη διατροφή
	me pleeree dheeatrofee
Is breakfast included?	Το πρωινό περιλαμβάνεται στην τιμή;
	to proeeno pereelamvanete steen teemee?

YOU MAY HEAR...

| Είμαστε γεμάτοι | We're full |
| eemaste yematee | |

56

Hotel (desk)

•••

Most hotels will provide breakfast if you ask for it.

I booked a room...	**Έκλεισα ένα δωμάτιο...**
	ekleesa **e**na dhom**a**teeo...
in the name of...	**στο όνομα...**
	sto **o**noma...
I'd like to see the room	**Θα ήθελα να δω το δωμάτιο**
	tha **ee**thela na dho to dhom**a**teeo
Where can I park?	**Πού μπορώ να παρκάρω;**
	poo bor**o** na park**a**ro?
What time is...?	**Τι ώρα σερβίρεται...;**
	tee **o**ra serv**ee**rete...?
dinner	**το δείπνο**
	to dh**ee**pno
breakfast	**το πρωινό**
	to proeen**o**
The key, please	**Το κλειδί, παρακαλώ**
	to kleedh**ee**, parakal**o**
room number...	**αριθμός δωματίου...**
	areethm**o**s dhomat**ee**oo...
Can you keep it in the safe, please?	**Μπορείτε να το φυλάξετε στο σέιφ;**
	bor**ee**te na to feel**a**ksete sto s**a**fe?

I'm leaving tomorrow	**Φεύγω αύριο**
	fevgho avreeo
Please prepare the bill	**Παρακαλώ ετοιμάστε το λογαριασμό**
	parakalo eteemaste to logharyasmo
Can I leave my luggage until...?	**Μπορώ να αφήσω τις βαλίτσες μου μέχρι...;**
	boro na afeeso tees valeetses moo mekhree...?

Hotel (room service)

. . . .

Come in!	**Περάστε!**
	peraste!
I'd like breakfast in my room	**Θα ήθελα το πρωινό στο δωμάτιο**
	tha eethela to proeeno sto dhomateeo
Please bring me...	**Παρακαλώ φέρτε μου...**
	parakalo ferte moo...
a glass	**ένα ποτήρι**
	ena poteeree
clean towels	**καθαρές πετσέτες**
	kathares petsetes
toilet paper	**χαρτί υγείας**
	khartee eeyeeas

I'd like an early morning call tomorrow	**Θα ήθελα να με ξυπνήσετε νωρίς το πρωί**
	tha **ee**thela na me kseepn**ee**sete nor**ee**s to pro**ee**
at 6 o'clock	**στις έξι η ώρα**
	stees **e**ksee ee **o**ra
I'd like an outside line	**Θα ήθελα μία εξωτερική γραμμή**
	tha **ee**thela m**ee**a eksotereek**ee** ghram**ee**
This doesn't work	**Δε δουλεύει αυτό**
	dhe dhool**e**vee aft**o**

Camping

Although camping is not as popular as in some other European countries, Greece has a number of campsites operated by the Greek Tourist Organisation. There are six campsites on Cyprus. In both countries camping is only permitted on official sites.

| Is there a restaurant on the campsite? | **Υπάρχει εστιατόριο στο κάμπινγκ;** |
| | eep**a**rkhee esteeat**o**reeo sto c**a**mping? |

Do you have any vacancies?	**Έχετε ελεύθερες θέσεις;** **e**khete el**e**ftheres th**e**sees?
Are showers.../ Is hot water.../ Is electricity...	**Οι ντουσιέρες…/το ζεστό νερό…/το ηλεκτρικό…** ee doosy**e**res…/to zest**o** ner**o**…/ to eelektreek**o**…
…included in the price?	**…περιλαμβάνονται στην τιμή;** …pereelamv**a**nonde steen teem**ee**?
We'd like to stay for ... nights	**Θέλουμε να μείνουμε … νύχτες** th**e**loome na m**ee**noome … n**ee**khtes
How much is it per night...?	**Πόσο κοστίζει τη νύχτα…;** p**o**so kost**ee**zee tee n**ee**khta…?
for a tent	**η σκηνή** ee skeen**ee**
per person	**το άτομο** to **a**tomo

Self-catering

....

Who do we contact if there are problems?	**Σε ποιόν θ' απευθυνθούμε αν υπάρξουν προβλήματα;** se pyon th-apeftheenth**oo**me an eep**a**rksoon provl**ee**mata?
How does the heating work?	**Πώς λειτουργεί η θέρμανση;** pos leetooryee ee th**e**rmansee?
Is there always hot water?	**Έχει πάντα ζεστό νερό;** **e**khee p**a**nta zest**o** ner**o**?
Where is the nearest supermarket?	**Πού είναι το κοντινότερο supermarket;** poo **ee**ne to kondeen**o**tero supermarket?
Where do we leave the rubbish?	**Που πετάμε τα σκουπίδια;** poo pet**a**me ta skoop**ee**dhya?

> **Sightseeing and tourist office** (p 72)

Self-catering

Shopping

Shopping phrases

• •

ΤΑΜΕΙΟ tam**ee**o	cash desk
ΕΔΩ ΠΛΗΡΩΝΕΤΕ edh**o** pleer**o**nete	pay here

FACE TO FACE

A **Τί θα θέλατε;**
tee tha th**e**late?
What would you like?

B **Έχετε...;**
ekhete...?
Do you have...?

A **Ναι, φυσικά. Θα θέλατε τίποτε άλλο;**
ne, feeseek**a**. Tha th**e**late t**ee**pote **a**llo?
Yes, certainly. Would you like anything else?

Where is...?	Πού είναι...;
	poo **ee**ne...?
Do you sell...?	Πουλάτε...;
	pool**a**te...?
I'm looking for	ψάχνω για ένα δώρο για...
a present for...	ps**a**khno ya **e**na dh**o**ro ya...
my mother	τη μητέρα μου
	tee meet**e**ra moo
a child	ένα παιδί
	ena pedh**ee**
Where can I	Πού μπορώ να αγοράσω...;
buy...?	poo bor**o** na aghor**a**so...?
toys	παιχνίδια
	pekhn**ee**dhya
gifts	δώρα
	dh**o**ra
It's too expensive	Είναι πολύ ακριβό
	eene pol**ee** akreev**o**
Have you	Έχετε τίποτε άλλο;
anything else?	**e**khete t**ee**pote **a**lo?

63

Shops

• •

baker's	ΑΡΤΟΠΟΙΕΙΟ	artopee-**ee**o
bookshop	ΒΙΒΛΙΟΠΩΛΕΙΟ	veevleeopol**ee**o
butcher's	ΚΡΕΟΠΩΛΕΙΟ	kreopol**ee**o
cake shop	ΖΑΧΑΡΟ–ΠΛΑΣΤΕΙΟ	zakharoplast**ee**o
clothes	ΕΝΔΥΜΑΤΑ	endh**ee**mata
gifts	ΔΩΡΑ	dh**o**ra
grocer's	ΠΑΝΤΟΠΩΛΕΙΟ	pantopol**ee**o
hairdresser's	ΚΟΜΜΩΤΗΡΙΟ	komotee**ree**o
pharmacy	ΦΑΡΜΑΚΕΙΟ	farmak**ee**o
shoe shop	ΚΑΤΑΣΤΗΜΑ ΥΠΟΔΗΜΑΤΩΝ	kat**a**steema eepodheem**a**ton
shop	ΚΑΤΑΣΤΗΜΑ	kat**a**steema
stationer's	ΧΑΡΤΟΠΩΛΕΙΟ	khartopol**ee**o
supermarket	ΣΟΥΠΕΡΜΑΡΚΕΤ	s**u**permarket
toy shop	ΠΑΙΧΝΙΔΙΑ	pekhn**ee**dheea

Food (general)

• •

biscuits	τα μπισκότα	beesk**o**ta
bread	το ψωμί	psom**ee**
butter	το βούτυρο	v**oo**teero
cheese	το τυρί	teer**ee**
chicken	το κοτόπουλο	kot**o**poolo

coffee (instant)	το Νεσκαφέ®	Nescafe
crisps	τα πατατάκια	patatakya
eggs	τα αβγά	avgha
ham	το ζαμπόν	zambon
honey	το μέλι	melee
jam	η μαρμελάδα	marmeladha
marmalade	η μαρμελάδα πορτοκάλι	marmeladha portokalee
milk	το γάλα	ghala
olive oil	το ελαιόλαδο	eleoladho
orange juice	ο χυμός πορτοκαλιού	kheemos portokalyoo
pepper	το πιπέρι	peeperee
salt	το αλάτι	alatee
sugar	η ζάχαρη	zakharee
tea	το τσάι	tsaee
vinegar	το ξύδι	kseedhee
yoghurt	το γιαούρτι	yaoortee

Food (fruit and veg)

••••••••••••••••••••••••••••••••••••••

Fruit

apples	τα μήλα	meela
apricots	τα βερίκοκα	vereekoka
bananas	οι μπανάνες	bananes

> **Measurements and quantities** (p 107) 65

cherries	τα κεράσια	ker**a**sya
figs	τα σύκα	s**ee**ka
grapefruit	τα γκρέιπφρουτ	gr**a**pefruit
grapes	τα σταφύλια	staf**ee**lya
lemon	το λεμόνι	lem**o**nee
melon	το πεπόνι	pep**o**nee
oranges	τα πορτοκάλια	portok**a**lya
peaches	τα ροδάκινα	rodh**a**keena
pears	τα αχλάδια	akhl**a**dhya
strawberries	οι φράουλες	fr**a**ooles
watermelon	το καρπούζι	karp**oo**zee

Vegetables

asparagus	τα σπαράγγια	spar**a**nghya
carrots	τα καρότα	kar**o**ta
cauliflower	το κουνουπίδι	koonoop**ee**dhee
courgettes	τα κολοκυθάκια	kolokeeth**a**kya
cucumber	το αγγούρι	ang**oo**ree
garlic	το σκόρδο	sk**o**rdho
lettuce	το μαρούλι	mar**oo**lee
mushrooms	τα μανιτάρια	maneet**a**rya
onions	τα κρεμμύδια	krem**ee**dhya
peas	ο αρακάς	arak**a**s
peppers	οι πιπεριές	peeper**ye**s
potatoes	οι πατάτες	pat**a**tes
spinach	το σπανάκι	span**a**kee
tomatoes	οι ντομάτες	dom**a**tes

Clothes

The Greek for size is **νούμερο** (n**oo**mero).

women's sizes		men's suit sizes		shoe sizes			
UK	EU	UK	EU	UK	EU	UK	EU
8	36	36	46	2	35	7	41
10	38	38	48	3	36	8	42
12	40	40	50	4	37	9	43
14	42	42	52	5	38	10	44
16	44	44	54	6	39	11	45
18	46	46	56				

FACE TO FACE

A **Μπορώ να το δοκιμάσω;**
bor**o** na to dhokeem**a**so?
May I try this on?

B **Ναι, φυσικά**
ne, feeseek**a**
Yes, of course

A **Έχετε μεγαλύτερο/μικρότερο νούμερο;**
ekhete meghal**ee**tero/meekr**o**tero n**oo**mero?
Do you have a larger/smaller size?

B **Τι νούμερο φοράτε;**
tee n**oo**mero for**a**te?
What size do you take?

Where are the changing rooms?	Πού είναι τα δοκιμαστήρια;	poo eene ta dhokeemasteereea?
Do you have this...?	έχετε αυτό...;	ekhete afto...?
in my size	στο νούμερο μου	sto noomero moo
in other colours	σε άλλα χρώματα	se ala khromata
I'm just looking	Απλώς κοιτάζω	aplos keetazo
I'll take it	Θα το πάρω	tha to paro

Clothes (articles)

coat	το παλτό	palto
dress	το φόρεμα	forema
jacket	η ζακέτα	zaketa
pyjamas	οι πυτζάμες	peetzames
shirt	το πουκάμισο	pookameeso
shorts	το σορτς	sorts
skirt	η φούστα	foosta
socks	οι κάλτσες	kaltses
suit	το κοστούμι	kostoomee

> **Paying** (p 89)

swimsuit	**το μαγιό**	mayo
top	**η μπλούζα**	blooza
trousers	**το παντελόνι**	pandelonee
t-shirt	**το μπλουζάκι**	bloozakee

Maps and guides

• •

You can buy maps and newspapers at kiosks in the big cities.

Have you...?	**Έχετε…;**
	ekhete...?
a map of the town	**ένα χάρτη της πόλης**
	ena kh**a**rtee tees p**o**lees
Can you show me (name of place) on the map?	**Μπορείτε να μου δείξετε … πάνω στο χάρτη;**
	bor**ee**te na moo dh**ee**ksete … p**a**no sto kh**a**rtee?
Have you...?	**Έχετε…;**
	ekhete...?
a guide book	**έναν οδηγό**
	enan odheegh**o**
in English	**στα αγγλικά**
	sta angleek**a**

> **Asking the way** (p 27) > **Sightseeing** (p 72)

| Do you have any English newspapers/ English books? | **Μήπως έχετε αγγλικές εφημερίδες/αγγλικά βιβλία;** m**ee**pos **e**khete angleek**e**s efeemer**ee**dhes/angleek**a** veevl**ee**a? |

Post office

Opening hours of post offices in Greece vary from place to place and according to the time of year. However, most of them close at midday, apart from those in major cities.

ΤΑΧΥΔΡΟΜΕΙΟ takheedhrom**ee**o	post office
ΓΡΑΜΜΑΤΟΣΗΜΑ ghramat**o**seema	stamps

Do you sell stamps?	**Πουλάτε γραμματόσημα;** pool**a**te ghramat**o**seema?
Is there a post office near here?	**Υπάρχει ταχυδρομείο εδώ κοντά;** eep**a**rkhee takheedhrom**ee**o edh**o** kond**a**?
Stamps for postcards to Great Britain	**Γραμματόσημα για κάρτες για τη Μεγάλη Βρετανία** ghramat**o**seema ya k**a**rtes ya tee megh**a**lee vretan**ee**a

70

Photos

....

Although cassettes for camcorders and memory
cards for digital cameras can be bought in the major
towns, if you are staying in a more remote area it is
wise to take enough film/memory cards and
cassettes for your requirements.

Have you batteries...?	Έχετε μπαταρίες...;
	ekhete batar**ee**-es...?
for this camera/ camcorder	γι'αυτή τη φωτογραφική μηχανή/βιντεοκάμερα
	yaft**ee** tee fotoghrafeek**ee** meekhan**ee**/video**c**amera
Can you develop this film?	Μπορείτε να εμφανίσετε αυτό το φιλμ;
	bor**ee**te na emfan**ee**sete aft**o** to feelm?
How much will it be?	Πόσο θα κοστίσει;
	p**o**so tha kost**ee**see?
Would you take a picture of us, please?	Μπορείτε να μας τραβήξετε μία φωτογραφία, παρακαλώ;
	bor**ee**te na mas trav**ee**ksete m**ee**a fotoghraf**ee**a parakal**o**?

> **Numbers** (p 109)

Leisure

Sightseeing and tourist office

The Greek Tourist Organisation (**EOT**) has offices in the larger towns in Greece, as does the Cyprus Tourism Organisation (**KOT**) in Cyprus. If you are looking for somewhere to stay, they should have details of hotels and campsites as well as of transport, local sights and events.

Leisure

Where is the tourist office?	Πού είναι το τουριστικό γραφείο; poo **ee**ne to tooreesteek**o** ghraf**ee**o?
What can we visit in the area?	Τι μπορούμε να δούμε σ' αυτή την περιοχή; tee bor**oo**me na dh**oo**me saft**ee** teen pereeokh**ee**?
When can we visit...?	Πότε μπορούμε να επισκεφθούμε...; pote bor**oo**me na epeeskefth**oo**me...?

the church	την εκκλησία
	teen eklees**ee**a
the museum	το μουσείο
	to moos**ee**o
Are there any excursions?	Γίνονται εκδρομές;
	y**ee**nonte ekdhrom**e**s?
How much does the entrance cost?	Πόσο κάνει η είσοδος;
	p**o**so k**a**nee ee **ee**sodhos?
Are there any reductions for...?	Γίνεται έκπτωση για...;
	y**ee**nete **e**kptosee ya...?
children	παιδιά
	pedhy**a**
students	φοιτητές
	feeteet**e**s
senior citizens	ηλικιωμένους
	eeleekeeom**e**noos

> **Maps and guides** (p 69) > **Leisure** (p 75)

Entertainment

....

Details of entertainments can be found in
newspapers. Local tourist offices will also have
details of local festivals. **ATHINORAMA**, a listings
magazine, is available in English from kiosks in
Athens.

What is there to do in the evenings?	Τι μπορεί να κάνει κανείς τα βράδυα;
	tee bor**ee** na k**a**nee kan**ee**s ta vr**a**dheea?
Do you know what events are on this week?	Ξέρετε τι εκδηλώσεις γίνονται αυτή τη βδομάδα;
	ks**e**rete tee ekdheel**o**sees y**ee**nonde aft**ee** tee vdhom**a**dha?
Is there anything for children?	Υπάρχει τίποτε για παιδιά;
	eep**a**rkhee t**ee**pote ya pedhy**a**?

YOU MAY HEAR...

Η είσοδος περιλαμβάνει και ένα ποτό	The entry fee includes one free drink
ee **ee**sodhos pereelamv**a**nee ke **e**na pot**o**	

Leisure/interests

....

Where can I go...?	**Πού μπορώ να πάω για...;**
	poo bor**o** na p**a**o ya...?
fishing	**ψάρεμα**
	ps**a**rema
Is there a swimming pool?	**Υπάρχει πισίνα;**
	eep**a**rkhee pees**ee**na?
When can we hire bikes?	**Πότε μπορούμε να νοικιάσουμε ποδήλατα;**
	p**o**te bor**oo**me na neeky**a**soome podh**ee**lata?
How much is it...?	**Πόσο κοστίζει...;**
	p**o**so kost**ee**zee...?
per hour	**την ώρα**
	teen **o**ra
per day	**τη μέρα**
	tee m**e**ra

> **Beach** (p 77) > **Sport** (p 80) > **Walking** (p 81)   75

Music

....

Are there any good concerts on?	**Υπάρχει καμία καλή συναυλία;**
	eep**a**rkhee kam**ee**a kal**ee** seenavl**ee**a?
Where can I hear some Greek music and songs?	**Πού μπορώ να ακούσω ελληνική μουσική και τραγούδια;**
	p**oo** bor**o** na ak**oo**so eleeneek**ee** mooseek**ee** ke tragh**oo**dhya?

Beach

....

Is there a good beach near here?	**Υπάρχει μία καλή παραλία εδώ κοντά;**
	eep**a**rkhee m**ee**a kal**ee** paral**ee**a edh**o** kond**a**?
sandy	**με άμμο**
	me **a**mo
Can I get there...?	**Μπορώ να πάω εκεί..;**
	bor**o** na p**a**o ek**ee**...?
by bus	**με λεωφορείο**
	me leofor**ee**o
by car	**με αυτοκίνητο**
	me aftok**ee**neeto
Does it have...?	**Έχει...;**
	ekhee...?
toilets	**τουαλέτες**
	tooal**e**tes
a restaurant	**εστιατόριο**
	esteeat**o**reeo
Can I hire...?	**Μπορώ να νοικιάσω...;**
	bor**o** na neeky**a**so...?
a deckchair	**μια ξαπλώστρα**
	mya ksapl**o**stra
an umbrella	**μια ομπρέλα**
	mya ombr**e**la

Beach

> **Making friends** (p 23) > **Leisure** (p 75)   77

Theatre/opera

Leisure

Classical Greek plays are performed at the Theatre of Herod Atticus at the foot of the Acropolis in Athens, at the theatre at Epidavros in the Peloponnese and elsewhere. It helps enormously if you buy an English translation of the play from a Greek bookshop and read it first to familiarise yourself with the plot. Hint: if you are planning to spend several hours sitting on a stone seat, take a cushion.

What's on at the theatre?	**Τι παίζει το θέατρο;** tee p**e**zee to th**e**atro?
How do we get to the theatre?	**Πώς θα πάμε στο θέατρο;** pos tha p**a**me sto th**e**atro?
What prices are the tickets?	**Τι τιμές έχουν τα εισιτήρια;** tee teem**e**s **e**khoon ta eeseet**ee**reea?
Two tickets...	**Δύο εισιτήρια…** dh**ee**o eeseet**ee**reea…
for tonight	**για απόψε** ya ap**o**pse
for tomorrow night	**για αύριο βράδυ** ya **a**vreeo vr**a**dhee
When does the performance begin?	**Πότε αρχίζει η παράσταση;** p**o**te arkh**ee**zee ee par**a**stasee?

| When does the performance end? | Πότε τελειώνει η παράσταση; |
| | pote teleeonee ee parastasee? |

Television

. . . .

Where is the television/ the video?	Πού είναι η τηλεόραση/ το βίντεο;
	poo eene ee teeleorasee/ to veedeo?
How do you switch it on?	Από πού ανάβει;
	apo poo anavee?
Please lower the volume	Χαμηλώνετε παρακαλώ τη φωνή
	khameelonete parakalo tee fonee
May I turn the volume up?	Μπορώ να δυναμώσω τη φωνή;
	boro na dheenamoso tee fonee?
When is the news?	Πότε έχει ειδήσεις;
	pote ekhee eedheesees?
Do you have any English-language channels?	Έχετε αγγλόφωνα κανάλια;
	ekhete anglofona kanalya?

Sport

....

Where can I...?	**Πού μπορώ να...;**
	poo bor**o** na...?
play tennis	**παίξω τένις**
	p**e**kso t**e**nees
go swimming	**κολυμπήσω**
	koleemb**ee**so
go jogging	**κάνω τζόκινγκ**
	k**a**no j**o**gging
go for a walk	**κάνω μία βόλτα**
	k**a**no m**ee**a v**o**lta
How much is it per hour?	**Πόσο κοστίζει την ώρα;**
	p**o**so kost**ee**zee teen **o**ra?
Can I hire...?	**Μπορώ να νοικιάσω...;**
	bor**o** na neeky**a**so...?
rackets	**ρακέτες**
	rak**e**tes

Leisure

Walking

....

Are there any guided walks?	Γίνονται καθόλου οργανωμένοι περίπατοι; yeenonte katholoo orghanomenee pereepatee?
Are there any special walking routes?	Υπάρχουν κάποιες ειδικές διαδρομές περιπάτου; eeparkhoon kapee-es eedheekes dheeadhromes pereepatoo?
How many kilometres is the walk?	Πόσα χιλιόμετρα είναι ο περίπατος; posa kheelyometra eene o pereepatos?
We'd like to go mountain climbing	Θα θέλαμε να κάνουμε ορειβασία tha thelame na kanoome oreevaseea

> **Maps and guides** (p 69)

Walking

Communications

Telephone and mobile

•••

To phone Greece from the UK, the international code is **00 30** followed by the Greek area code, e.g. Athens **210**, and the phone number you require. For Cyprus, dial **00 357** followed by the Cyprus area code, e.g. Nicosia **2**, Limassol **5**, and the phone number.

FACE TO FACE

A Παρακαλώ/Ναι
parakal**o**/Ne
Hello

B Θα ήθελα να μιλήσω στον/στην...
tha **ee**thela na meel**ee**so ston/steen...
I'd like to speak to...

A Ποιός είστε;
py**o**s **ee**ste?
Who's calling?

B **Είμαι η Μαρία**
eeme ee Maria
It's Maria

A **Ένα λεπτό…/Περιμένετε, παρακαλώ**
ena lepto…/pereemenete, parakalo
Just a moment…/Hold on, please

I want to make a phone call	**Θέλω να κάνω ένα τηλεφώνημα** thelo na kano ena teelefoneema
Where can I buy a phonecard?	**Πού μπορώ να αγοράσω μία τηλεκάρτα;** poo boro na aghoraso meea teelekarta?
A phonecard, please	**Μία τηλεκάρτα, παρακαλώ** meea teelekarta, parakalo
Do you have a mobile?	**Έχετε κινητό (τηλέφωνο);** ekhete keeneeto (teelefono)?
What is the number of your mobile?	**Ποιός είναι ο αριθμός του κινητού σας (τηλεφώνου);** pyos eene o areethmos too keeneetoo sas (teelefonoo)?
My mobile number is…	**Ο αριθμός του κινητού μου (τηλεφώνου) είναι…** o areethmos too keeneetoo moo (teelefonoo) eene…

Mr...	**Τον κύριο...**
	ton k**ee**reeo...
Mrs/Ms...,	**Την κυρία..., παρακαλώ**
please	teen keer**ee**a..., parakal**o**
Extension	**εσωτερική γραμμή**
number	esotereek**ee** ghram**ee**

Πήρατε λάθος αριθμό	You've got the wrong
p**ee**rate **l**athos areethm**o**	number
Αφήστε το μήνυμά	Leave a message after
σας μετά από το	the tone
χαρακτηριστικό ήχο	
af**ee**ste to m**ee**neem**a** sas	
met**a** ap**o** to	
kharakteereesteek**o ee**kho	
Παρακαλούμε να	Please switch off all
κλείσετε τα κινητά	mobiles
τηλέφωνα	
parakal**oo**me na kl**ee**sete ta	
keeneet**a** teel**e**fona	

Communications

84

E-mail

∙∙∙∙∙∙∙∙∙∙∙∙∙∙∙∙∙∙∙∙∙∙∙∙∙∙∙∙∙∙∙∙∙∙∙

Although you will hear the English word e-mail
used, the proper Greek term for e-mail address is
η ηλεκτρονική διεύθυνση (ee eelektroneek**ee**
dhee-**e**ftheensee).

Do you have e-mail?	**Έχετε e-mail;** **e**khete e-mail?
How do you spell it?	**Πώς γράφεται;** p**o**s ghr**a**fete?
Did you get my e-mail?	**Πήρατε το e-mail μου;** p**ee**rate to e-mail moo?
My e-mail address is...	**Η e-mail διεύθυνσή μου είναι...** ee e-mail dhee-**e**ftheens**ee** moo **ee**ne...

Internet

It is usually easy to find an internet café where you can check your e-mail messages, etc. National and local tourist information can also be accessed via the internet. Greek websites have the suffix **.gr**.

Are there any internet cafés here?	**Υπάρχουν internet café στην περιοχή;** eep**a**rkhoon internet kaf**e** steen pereeokh**ee**?
How much does it cost...?	**Πόσο κοστίζει...;** p**o**so kost**ee**zee...?
for one hour	**για μια ώρα** ya mya **o**ra

Fax

....

To fax Greece from the UK, the international code is
00 30 followed by the Greek area code, e.g. Athens
210, and the fax number. For Cyprus, dial **00 357**
followed by the Cyprus area code, e.g. Nicosia **2**,
Limassol **5**, and the fax number.

Addressing a fax

....

ΑΠΟ	from
ΥΠ' ΟΨΙΝ	for the attention of
ΗΜΕΡΟΜΗΝΙΑ	date
ΘΕΜΑ	re

Do you have a fax?	**Έχετε φαξ;**
	ekhete fax?
What is your fax number?	**Ποιός είναι ο αριθμός του φαξ σας;**
	py**o**s **ee**ne o areethm**o**s too fax sas?
I want to send a fax	**Θέλω να στείλω ένα φαξ**
	th**e**lo na st**ee**lo **e**na fax

Practicalities

Money

Banks in Greece and Cyprus are generally open only during the morning (Greece: 8.30 am–1 pm, Cyprus 8.30 am–12 noon), although in tourist areas some may open outside these hours.

ΤΡΑΠΕΖΑ trapeza	bank
ΠΙΣΤΩΤΙΚΕΣ ΚΑΡΤΕΣ peestoteekes kartes	credit cards

Where can I change some money?	Πού μπορώ να αλλάξω χρήματα; poo boro na alakso khreemata?
Where is the nearest bank?	Πού είναι η κοντινότερη τράπεζα; poo eene ee kondeenoteree trapeza?
I want to change these traveller's cheques	Θέλω να αλλάξω αυτές τις ταξιδιωτικές επιταγές thelo na alakso aftes tees takseedhyoteekes epeetayes

When does the bank open?	Πότε ανοίγει η τράπεζα;
	pote aneeyee ee trapeza?
When does the bank close?	Πότε κλείνει η τράπεζα;
	pote kleenee ee trapeza?

Paying

ευρώ evro	euro
λεπτά lepta	cents
ΛΟΓΑΡΙΑΣΜΟΣ loghareeasmos	bill
ΤΑΜΕΙΟ tameeo	cash desk
ΤΙΜΟΛΟΓΙΟ teemoloyeeo	invoice
ΑΠΟΔΕΙΞΗ apodheeksee	receipt

How much is it?	Πόσο κάνει;
	poso kanee?
Can I pay...?	Μπορώ να πληρώσω...;
	boro na pleeroso...?
by credit card	με πιστωτική κάρτα
	me peestoteekee karta
by cheque	με τσεκ
	me tsek
Do you take credit cards?	Παίρνετε πιστωτικές κάρτες;
	pernete peestoteekes kartes?

Put it on my bill	Βάλτε το στο λογαριασμό μου
	valte to sto logharyasmo moo
I need a receipt	Χρειάζομαι απόδειξη
	khreeazome apodheeksee
Do I pay in advance?	Προπληρώνω;
	propleerono?
Where do I pay?	Πού πληρώνω;
	poo pleerono?

Luggage

My luggage hasn't arrived	Οι αποσκευές μου δεν έφτασαν
	ee aposkeves moo dhen eftasan
My suitcase has arrived damaged	Η βαλίτσα μου έφτασε χαλασμένη
	ee valeetsa moo eftase khalasmenee
Can I leave my luggage here?	Μπορώ να αφήσω εδώ τις αποσκευές μου;
	boro na afeeso edho tees aposkeves moo?

Μπορείτε να τις αφήσετε εδώ μέχρι τις 6 η ώρα
bor**ee**te na tees af**ee**sete edh**o** m**e**khree tees **e**ksee ee **o**ra

You may leave it here until 6 o'clock

Repairs

This is broken	Έσπασε αυτό **e**spase aft**o**
Where can I get this repaired?	Πού θα μου το επισκευάσουν; poo tha moo to epeeskev**a**soon?
Is it worth repairing?	Αξίζει τον κόπο να επισκευαστεί; aks**ee**zee ton k**o**po na epeeskevast**ee**?
Can you repair...?	Μπορείτε να επισκευάσετε...; bor**ee**te na epeeskev**a**sete...?
these shoes	αυτά τα παπούτσια aft**a** ta pap**oo**tsya
my watch	το ρολόι μου o rolo**ee** moo

Laundry

. . . .

You can get clothes washed or dry-cleaned at laundries in Greece. Self-service launderettes do not exist.

ΚΑΘΑΡΙΣΤΗΡΙΟ kathareest**ee**reeo	dry-cleaner's

Where can I do some washing?	Πού μπορώ να πλύνω μερικά ρούχα; poo bor**o** na pl**ee**no mereek**a** r**oo**kha?
Is there a dry-cleaner's near here?	Υπάρχει καθαριστήριο εδώ κοντά; eep**a**rkhee kathareest**ee**reeo edh**o** kond**a**?

Complaints

. . . .

This doesn't work	Δε δουλεύει αυτό dhe dhoolevee aft**o**
The ... doesn't work	ο/η/το ... δε δουλεύει o/ee/to ... dhe dhool**e**vee
The ... don't work	οι/τα ... δε δουλεύουν ee/ta ... dhe dhool**e**voon

lights	τα φώτα
	ta f**o**ta
heating	η θέρμανση
	ee th**e**rmansee
air conditioning	ο κλιματισμός
	o kleemateesm**o**s
This is dirty	Αυτό είναι βρώμικο
	aft**o** **ee**ne vr**o**meeko
There's a problem with the room	Υπάρχει πρόβλημα με το δωμάτιο
	eep**a**rkhee pr**o**vleema me to dhom**a**teeo
It's noisy	Έχει θόρυβο
	ekhee th**o**reevo
I want a refund	Θέλω τα χρήματά μου πίσω
	th**e**lo ta khr**ee**mat**a** moo p**ee**so

Problems

Can you help me?	Μπορείτε να με βοηθήσετε;
	bor**ee**te na me voeeth**ee**sete?
I only speak a little Greek	Μιλάω μόνο λίγα ελληνικά
	meel**a**o m**o**no l**ee**gha eleeneek**a**
Does anyone here speak English?	Μιλά κανείς εδώ αγγλικά;
	meel**a** kan**ee**s edh**o** angleek**a**?

93

I would like to speak to whoever is in charge	Θα ήθελα να μιλήσω στον υπεύθυνο tha **ee**thela na meel**ee**so ston eep**e**ftheeno
I'm lost	Έχω χαθεί **e**kho khath**ee**
How do I get to...?	Πώς θα πάω στο...; p**o**s tha p**a**o sto...?
I've missed...	Έχασα… **e**khasa...
my bus	το λεωφορείο μου to leofor**ee**o moo
my plane	το αεροπλάνο μου to aeropl**a**no moo
Can you show me how this works?	Μπορείτε να μου δείξετε πώς δουλεύει αυτό; bor**ee**te na moo dh**ee**ksete pos dhool**e**vee aft**o**?
I have lost my purse	Έχασα το πορτοφόλι μου **e**khasa to portof**o**lee moo
I need to get to...	Πρέπει να φτάσω στο… pr**e**pee na ft**a**so sto...

Emergencies

. . . .

The emergency numbers in Greece (for Athens) are POLICE **100**, AMBULANCE **166** and FIRE **199**. In Cyprus the emergency number for all these services is **199**.

ΑΣΤΥΝΟΜΙΑ asteenom**ee**a	police
ΑΣΘΕΝΟΦΟΡΟ astheno**fo**ro	ambulance
ΠΥΡΟΣΒΕΣΤΙΚΗ peerosvesteek**ee**	fire brigade

Help!	Βοήθεια! vo**ee**theea!
Fire!	Φωτιά! foty**a**!
Can you help me?	Μπορείτε να με βοηθήσετε; bor**ee**te na me voeeth**ee**sete?
There's been an accident!	Έγινε ατύχημα! **e**yeene at**ee**kheema!
Someone is injured	Κάποιος τραυματίστηκε k**a**pyos travmat**ee**steeke
Someone has been knocked down by a car	Κάποιον χτύπησε ένα αυτοκίνητο k**a**pyon kht**ee**peese **e**na aftok**ee**neeto

95

Call...	Φωνάξτε...
	fon**a**kste...
the police	την αστυνομία
	teen asteenom**ee**a
an ambulance	ένα ασθενοφόρο
	ena asthenof**o**ro
please	παρακαλώ
	parakal**o**
Where is the police station?	Πού είναι το αστυνομικό τμήμα;
	p**oo ee**ne to asteenomeek**o** tm**ee**ma?
I've been robbed	Με έκλεψαν
	me **e**klepsan
I want to report a theft	Θέλω να αναφέρω μια κλοπή
	th**e**lo na anaf**e**ro mya klop**ee**
My car has been stolen	Μου έκλεψαν το αυτοκίνητο
	moo **e**klepsan to aftok**ee**neeto
Someone's stolen my...	Κάποιος μου έκλεψε...
	k**a**pyos moo **e**klepse...
...bag	...την τσάντα
	...teen ts**a**nda
...traveller's cheques	...τις ταξιδιωτικές επιταγές
	...tees takseedheeoteek**e**s epeeta-y**e**s

96

My car has been broken into	Μου παραβίασαν το αυτοκίνητο
	moo parav**ee**asan to aftok**ee**neeto
I've been attacked	Μου επιτέθηκαν
	moo epeet**e**theekan
I've been raped	Με βίασαν
	me v**ee**asan
I want to speak to a policewoman	Θέλω να μιλήσω σε γυναίκα αστυνομικό
	th**e**lo na meel**ee**so se yeen**e**ka asteenomeek**o**
I need to make an urgent telephone call	Πρέπει να κάνω ένα επείγον τηλεφώνημα
	pr**e**pee na k**a**no **e**na ep**ee**ghon teelef**o**neema
I need a report for my insurance	Θέλω μια αναφορά για την ασφαλιστική μου εταιρεία
	th**e**lo mya anafor**a** ya teen asfaleesteek**ee** moo eter**ee**a
I didn't know the speed limit	Δεν ήξερα το όριο ταχύτητας
	dhen **ee**ksera to **o**reeo takh**ee**teetas
I'm very sorry	Λυπάμαι πολύ
	leep**a**me pol**ee**

How much is the fine?	Πόσο είναι το πρόστιμο;
	poso **ee**ne to pr**o**steemo?
Where do I pay it?	Πού θα το πληρώσω;
	poo tha to pleer**o**so?

| Περάσατε με κόκκινο | You went through a |
| per**a**sate me k**o**keeno | red light |

Health

Pharmacy

ΦΑΡΜΑΚΕΙΟ	farmak**ee**o	pharmacy/chemist
ΣΥΝΤΑΓΗ	seenday**ee**	prescription

I don't feel well	**Δεν αισθάνομαι καλά** dhen esth**a**nome kal**a**
Have you something for...?	**Έχετε τίποτε για...;** **e**khete t**ee**pote ya....?
sunburn	**τα εγκαύματα** ta eng**a**vmata
travel sickness	**τη ναυτία** tee naft**ee**a
diarrhoea	**τη διάρροια** tee dhee**a**reea
Is it safe for children?	**Είναι ασφαλές για παιδιά;** **ee**ne asfal**e**s ya pedy**a**?
How much should I give?	**Πόσο πρέπει να δώσω;** p**o**so pr**e**pee na dh**o**so?

Να το παίρνετε τρεις φορές την ημέρα πριν/με/μετά το φαγητό na to **pe**rnete trees for**e**s teen eem**e**ra preen/me/met**a** to fayeet**o**	Take it three times a day before/with/ after meals

Doctor

....

ΝΟΣΟΚΟΜΕΙΟ nosokom**ee**o	hospital

FACE TO FACE

A Δεν νιώθω καλά
  then nee**o**tho kal**a**
  I don't feel very well

B Έχετε πυρετό;
  ekhete peeret**o**?
  Do you have a temperature?

A Όχι, πονάω εδώ...
  okhi, pon**a**o edh**o**...
  No, I have a pain here...

I need a doctor	Χρειάζομαι γιατρό
	khree**a**zome yatr**o**
My son is ill	Ο γιος μου είναι άρρωστος
	o yos moo **ee**ne **a**rostos
My daughter is ill	Η κόρη μου είναι άρρωστη
	ee k**o**ree moo **ee**ne **a**rostee
I'm pregnant	Είμαι έγγυος
	eeme **e**ngeeos
I'm diabetic	Είμαι διαβητικός(-ή)
	eeme dheeaveeteek-**o**s(-ee)
I'm allergic to penicillin	Έχω αλλεργία στην πενικιλλίνη
	ekho alery**ee**a steen peneekeel**ee**nee
My blood group is...	Η ομάδα αίματός μου είναι...
	ee om**a**dha **e**mat**o**s moo **ee**ne...
I've been stung by something	κάτι με τσίμπησε
	k**a**tee me ts**ee**embeese
Will he/she have to go to hospital?	Πρέπει να μπει στο νοσοκομείο;
	pr**e**pee na bee sto nosokom**ee**o?
I need a receipt for the insurance	Χρειάζομαι απόδειξη για την ασφαλιστική μου εταιρεία
	khree**a**zome ap**o**dheeksee ya teen asfaleesteek**ee** moo etere**ea**

101

Θα πρέπει να μπείτε στο νοσοκομείο tha pr**e**pee na b**ee**te sto nosokom**ee**o	You will have to go into hospital
Δεν είναι σοβαρό dhen **ee**ne sovar**o**	It's not serious

Dentist

I need a dentist	**Χρειάζομαι οδοντίατρο** khree**a**zome odhond**ee**atro
He/She has toothache	**Έχει πονόδοντο** **e**khee pon**o**dhondo
Can you do a temporary filling?	**Μπορείτε να κάνετε προσωρινό σφράγισμα;** bor**ee**te na k**a**nete prosoreen**o** sfr**a**-yeesma?
It hurts (me)	**Με πονάει** me pon**a**ee
Can you give me something for the pain?	**Μπορείτε να μου δώσετε κάτι για τον πόνο;** bor**ee**te na moo dh**o**sete k**a**tee ya ton p**o**no?
How much will it be?	**Πόσο θα κοστίσει;** p**o**so tha kost**ee**see?

Health

| I need a receipt for my insurance | **Χρειάζομαι απόδειξη για την ασφαλιστική μου εταιρεία** |
| | khree**a**zome ap**o**dheeksee ya teen asfaleesteek**ee** moo eter**ee**a |

| **Πρέπει να βγει** prepee na vyee | It has to come out |

> **Emergencies** (p 95)

Dentist

Different types of travellers

Disabled travellers

••

Facilities for the disabled are not as widely available in Greece and Cyprus as in the UK, although they are improving. It is worth checking with individual hotels etc. prior to booking. The new underground in Athens has superb facilities for the disabled.

What facilities do you have for disabled people?	Τι ευκολίες έχετε για άτομα με ειδικές ανάγκες; tee efkol**ee**-es **e**khete ya **a**toma me eedheek**e**s an**a**nges?
Are there any toilets for the disabled?	Υπάρχουν τουαλέτες για άτομα με ειδικές ανάγκες; eep**a**rkhoon tooal**e**tes ya **a**toma me eedheek**e**s an**a**nges?
Do you have any bedrooms on the ground floor?	Έχετε υπνοδωμάτια στο ισόγειο; **e**khete eepnodhom**a**teea sto ees**o**yeeo?
Is there a lift?	Υπάρχει ασανσέρ; eep**a**rkhee asans**e**r?

Where is the lift?	Πού είναι το ασανσέρ;
	p**oo ee**ne to asans**e**r?
How many stairs are there?	Πόσες σκάλες υπάρχουν;
	p**o**ses sk**a**les eep**a**rkhoon?
Do you have wheelchairs?	Έχετε καρότσια;
	ekhete kar**o**tsya?
Can you visit ... in a wheelchair?	Μπορεί κανείς να επισκεφτεί ... με καρότσι;
	bor**ee** kan**ee**s na epeeskeft**ee** ... me kar**o**tsee?
Where is the wheelchair-accessible entrance?	Πού είναι η είσοδος με πρόσβαση για τα καρότσια;
	p**oo ee**ne ee **ee**sodhos me pr**o**svasee ya ta kar**o**tsya?
Is there a reduction for disabled people?	Γίνεται έκπτωση στα άτομα με ειδικές ανάγκες;
	y**ee**nete **e**kptosee sta **a**toma me eedheek**e**s an**a**nges?

With kids

....

A child's ticket	Ένα παιδικό εισιτήριο
	ena pedhee**ko** eeseet**ee**reeo
He/She is ... years old	είναι ... χρονών
	eene ... khron**on**
Is there a reduction for children?	Υπάρχει ειδική τιμή για παιδιά;
	eep**a**rkhee eedheek**ee** teem**ee** ya pedhy**a**?
Is there a children's menu?	Υπάρχει παιδικό μενού;
	eep**a**rkhee pedhee**ko** men**oo**?
Have you...?	Έχετε...;
	ekhete...?
a high chair	μία παιδική καρέκλα
	m**ee**a pedheek**ee** kar**e**kla
a cot	ένα παιδικό κρεββάτι
	ena pedhee**ko** krev**a**tee
Is it ok to bring children?	Υπάρχει πρόβλημα αν φέρουμε τα παιδιά;
	eep**a**rkhee pro**v**leema an f**e**roome ta pedhy**a**?
Do you have children?	Έχετε παιδιά;
	ekhete pedhy**a**?

Reference

Measurements and quantities

....

Liquids

1/2 litre of...	**μισό λίτρο...**
	meeso leetro...
a litre of...	**ένα λίτρο...**
	ena leetro...
a bottle of...	**ένα μπουκάλι...**
	ena bookalee...
a glass of...	**ένα ποτήρι...**
	ena poteeree...

Weights

100 grams	**εκατό γραμμάρια**
	ekato ghramareea
1/2 kilo of... (500 g)	**μισό κιλό...**
	meeso keelo...
a kilo of... (1000 g)	**ένα κιλό...**
	ena keelo...

Food

a slice of...	**μια φέτα...**
	mya feta...
a portion of...	**μια μερίδα...**
	mya mereedha...
a box of...	**ένα κουτί...**
	ena kootee...
a packet of...	**ένα πακέτο...**
	ena paketo...
a tin of...	**μια κονσέρβα...**
	mya konserva...
a jar of...	**ένα βάζο...**
	ena vazo...

Miscellaneous

10 euros	**δέκα ευρώ**
	dheka evro
20 cents	**είκοσι λεπτά**
	eekosee lepta
a third	**ένα τρίτο**
	ena treeto
a quarter	**ένα τέταρτο**
	ena tetarto
ten per cent	**δέκα τοις εκατό**
	dheka tees ekato
more...	**περισσότερο...**
	pereesotero...

less...	**λιγότερο...**
	leegh**o**tero...
enough	**αρκετό**
	arket**o**
double	**διπλό**
	dheepl**o**
twice	**διπλάσιο**
	dheepl**a**seeo
three times	**τριπλάσιο**
	treepl**a**seeo

Numbers

....

0	**μηδέν** meedh**e**n
1	**ένα e**na
2	**δύο** dh**ee**o
3	**τρία** tr**ee**a
4	**τέσσερα** t**e**sera
5	**πέντε** p**e**nde
6	**έξι e**ksee
7	**εφτά** eft**a**
8	**οχτώ** okht**o**
9	**εννιά** eny**a**
10	**δέκα** dh**e**ka
11	**έντεκα e**ndeka
12	**δώδεκα** dh**o**dheka
13	**δεκατρία** dhekatr**ee**a

14	**δεκατέσσερα** dhekatesera
15	**δεκαπέντε** dhekapende
16	**δεκαέξι** dhekaeksee
17	**δεκαεφτά** dhekaefta
18	**δεκαοχτώ** dhekaokhto
19	**δεκαεννιά** dhekaenya
20	**είκοσι ee**kosee
21	**είκοσι ένα ee**kosee **e**na
22	**είκοσι δύο ee**kosee dh**ee**o
30	**τριάντα** treeanda
40	**σαράντα** saranda
50	**πενήντα** pen**ee**nda
60	**εξήντα** eks**ee**nda
70	**εβδομήντα** evdhom**ee**nda
80	**ογδόντα** oghdh**o**nda
90	**ενενήντα** enen**ee**nda
100	**εκατό** ekat**o**
110	**εκατόν δέκα** ekat**o**n dh**e**ka
500	**πεντακόσια** pendak**o**sya
1,000	**χίλια** kh**ee**lya
2,000	**δύο χιλιάδες** dh**ee**o kheelyadhes
1 million	**ένα εκατομμύριο e**na ekatom**ee**reeo

1st	**πρώτος**	6th	**έκτος**
	protos		ektos
2nd	**δεύτερος**	7th	**έβδομος**
	dhefteros		evdhomos
3rd	**τρίτος**	8th	**όγδοος**
	treetos		oghdho-os
4th	**τέταρτος**	9th	**ένατος**
	tetartos		enatos
5th	**πέμπτος**	10th	**δέκατος**
	pemptos		dhekatos

Days and months

Days

Monday	**Δευτέρα**	dheftera
Tuesday	**Τρίτη**	treetee
Wednesday	**Τετάρτη**	tetartee
Thursday	**Πέμπτη**	pemptee
Friday	**Παρασκευή**	paraskevee
Saturday	**Σάββατο**	savato
Sunday	**Κυριακή**	keeryakee

Months

January	**Ιανουάριος**	eeanoo**a**reeos
February	**Φεβρουάριος**	fevroo**a**reeos
March	**Μάρτιος**	m**a**rteeos
April	**Απρίλιος**	apr**ee**leeos
May	**Μάιος**	m**a**eeos
June	**Ιούνιος**	ee**oo**neeos
July	**Ιούλιος**	ee**oo**leeos
August	**Αύγουστος**	**av**ghoostos
September	**Σεπτέμβριος**	sept**e**mvreeos
October	**Οκτώβριος**	okt**o**vreeos
November	**Νοέμβριος**	no**e**mvreeos
December	**Δεκέμβριος**	dhek**e**mvreeos

Seasons

spring	**Άνοιξη**	**a**neeksee
summer	**Καλοκαίρι**	kalok**e**ree
autumn	**Φθινόπωρο**	ftheen**o**poro
winter	**Χειμώνας**	kheem**o**nas

What's the date?	**Τι ημερομηνία έχουμε;**
	tee eemeromeen**ee**a **e**khoome?
It's the 5th of August 2007	**Είναι η 5η Αυγούστου 2007**
	eene ee p**e**mptee avgh**oo**stoo dh**ee**o kheelee**a**des eft**a**

on Saturday	**το Σάββατο**	
	to s**a**vato	
on Saturdays	**τα Σάββατα**	
	ta s**a**vata	
this Saturday	**αυτό το Σάββατο**	
	aft**o** to s**a**vato	
next Saturday	**το επόμενο Σάββατο**	
	to ep**o**meno s**a**vato	
last Saturday	**το περασμένο Σάββατο**	
	to perasm**e**no s**a**vato	
in June	**τον Ιούνιο**	
	ton ee**oo**neeo	
at the beginning of June	**στις αρχές Ιουνίου**	
	stees arkh**e**s eeoon**ee**oo	
at the end of June	**στα τέλη Ιουνίου**	
	sta t**e**lee eeoon**ee**oo	
before summer	**πριν από το καλοκαίρι**	
	preen ap**o** to kalok**e**ree	
during the summer	**μέσα στο καλοκαίρι**	
	m**e**sa sto kalok**e**ree	
after summer	**μετά το καλοκαίρι**	
	met**a** to kalok**e**ree	

Time

••

When telling the time in Greek, remember that the hour comes first, then 'past' **και** (ke) or 'to' **παρά** (par**a**) and finally the minutes, e.g. 8.10 **οκτώ και δέκα** (okt**o** ke dh**e**ka) – ten past eight, 11.40 **δώδεκα παρά είκοσι** (dh**o**dheka par**a** ee**e**kosee) – twenty to twelve.

What time is it, please?	**Τι ώρα είναι, παρακαλώ;**
	tee **o**ra **e**ene, parakal**o**?
am	**πμ**
	preen to meseem**e**ree
pm	**μμ**
	met**a** to meseem**e**ree
It's...	**Είναι...**
	eene...
2 o'clock	**δύο η ώρα**
	dh**ee**o ee **o**ra
3 o'clock	**τρεις η ώρα**
	trees ee **o**ra
6 o'clock (etc.)	**έξι η ώρα**
	eksee ee **o**ra
It's 1 o'clock	**Είναι μία η ώρα**
	eene m**ee**a ee **o**ra
It's 1200	**Είναι δώδεκα**
	eene dh**o**dheka

114

midday	**το μεσημέρι**
	to meseem**e**ree
midnight	**τα μεσάνυχτα**
	ta mes**a**neekhta
9	**εννέα**
	en**e**a
9.10	**εννέα και δέκα**
	en**e**a ke dh**e**ka
quarter past 9	**εννέα και τέταρτο**
	en**e**a ke t**e**tarto
9.20	**εννέα και είκοσι**
	en**e**a ke **ee**kosee
9.30	**εννέα και μισή**
	en**e**a ke mees**ee**
9.35	**εννέα και τριάντα πέντε**
	en**e**a ke tree**a**nta p**e**nte
quarter to 10	**δέκα παρά τέταρτο**
	dh**e**ka par**a** t**e**tarto
10 to 10	**δέκα παρά δέκα**
	dh**e**ka par**a** dh**e**ka

Time phrases

••••••••••••••••••••••••••••••

When does it open/close?	**Πότε ανοίγει/κλείνει;**
	pote aneeyee/kleenee?
When does it begin/finish?	**Πότε αρχίζει/τελειώνει;**
	pote arkheezee/teleeonee?
at 3 o'clock	**στις τρεις η ώρα**
	stees trees ee ora
before 3 o'clock	**πριν από τις τρεις**
	preen apo tees trees
after 3 o'clock	**μετά τις τρεις**
	meta tees trees
today	**σήμερα**
	seemera
tonight	**απόψε**
	apopse
tomorrow	**αύριο**
	avreeo
yesterday	**χθες**
	khthes

Eating out

Eating places

ΜΠΑΡ (bar) Serves drinks and sometimes snacks.

ΚΑΦΕΤΕΡΙΑ (kafet**e**reea) Serves drinks, coffee, light meals, snacks.

ΤΑΒΕΡΝΑ (tav**e**rna) Either a traditional tavern or an establishment aimed at the tourist.

ΟΥΖΕΡΙ (oozer**ee**) A small bar serving ouzo and other traditional drinks. They may also serve mezedes.

ΣΟΥΒΛΑΤΖΙΔΙΚΟ (soovlatz**ee**dheeko) Take-aways selling mainly pork kebabs (soovl**a**kee) and chips.

ΚΑΦΕΝΕΙΟ (kafen**ee**o) Traditional coffee shop which is often a social centre for the men of a village.

ΕΣΤΙΑΤΟΡΙΟ (esteeat**o**reeo) Restaurant.

ΡΕΣΤΟΡΑΝ (restor**a**n) Restaurants in tourist resorts usually start serving food from midday or 1 pm until late at night. Greeks tend to have a large meal for lunch between 1 and 3 pm. If going out for dinner, they tend to do so after 8 or 9 pm.

ΖΑΧΑΡΟΠΛΑΣΤΕΙΟ (zakharoplast**ee**o) Patisserie selling sweet Greek pastries either to take away or to eat on the premises. It will usually also serve coffee and soft drinks.

In a bar/café

If you ask for a coffee you are likely to be served a Greek (Turkish) coffee. If you like it sweet ask for **καφέ γλυκό** (kaf**e** gleek**o**), medium sweet is **καφέ μέτριο** (kaf**e** m**e**treeo) and without sugar is **καφέ σκέτο** (kaf**e** sk**e**to). If you want an instant coffee you will need to ask for **ένα νεσκαφέ** (**e**na neskaf**e**). A refreshing drink in the summer is iced coffee. Ask for **καφέ φραπέ** (kaf**e** frap**e**).

A Τί θα πάρετε;
tee tha p**a**rete?
What will you have?

B Ένα τσάι με γάλα παρακαλώ
ena ts**a**ee me gh**a**la parakal**o**
A tea with milk, please

a cappuccino	ένα καπουτσίνο	**e**na kapoots**ee**no
a beer	μία μπύρα	m**ee**a b**ee**ra
an ouzo	ένα ούζο	**e**na o**u**zo
...please	...παρακαλώ	...parakal**o**
a tea...	ένα τσάι...	**e**na ts**a**ee...
with lemon	με λεμόνι	me lem**o**nee
without sugar	χωρίς ζάχαρη	khor**ee**s z**a**kharee
for me	για μένα	ya m**e**na
for her	γι' αυτήν	yaft**ee**n
for him	γι' αυτόν	yaft**o**n

for us	για μας
	ya mas
A bottle of	Ένα μπουκάλι
mineral water	εμφιαλωμένο νερό
	ena book**a**lee emfeealom**e**no
	ner**o**
sparkling	αεριούχο
	aeree**oo**kho
still	απλό
	apl**o**

Other drinks to try

ένα χυμό λεμονιού (**e**na kheem**o** lemony**oo**)
  a lemon juice

ένα χυμό πορτοκαλιού (**e**na kheem**o**
  portokaly**oo**) an orange juice

ένα ποτήρι ρετσίνα (**e**na pot**ee**ree rets**ee**na)
  a glass of retsina

ένα κονιάκ (**e**na kony**a**k) a brandy

ένα αναψυκτικό (**e**na anapseekteek**o**)
  a soft drink

Eating out

120

In a restaurant

A Θα ήθελα ένα τραπέζι για … άτομα
tha **ee**thela **e**na trap**e**zee ya … **a**toma
I'd like to book a table for … people

B Ναι, για πότε;
ne, ya p**o**te?
Yes, when for?

A για απόψε…/για αύριο βράδυ…
ya ap**o**pse…/ya **a**vreeo vr**a**dee…
For tonight…/For tomorrow night…

The menu, please	Τον κατάλογο, παρακαλώ
	ton kat**a**logho, parakal**o**
What is the dish of the day?	Ποιο είναι το πιάτο της ημέρας;
	pyo **ee**ne to py**a**to tees eem**e**ras?
Have you a set price menu?	Έχετε ένα προκαθορισμένο μενού;
	ekhete **e**na prokathoreesm**e**no men**oo**?
What is this?	Τι είναι αυτό;
	tee **ee**ne aft**o**?
I'll have this	Θα πάρω αυτό
	tha p**a**ro aft**o**
Excuse me!	Με συγχωρείτε!
	me seenkhor**ee**te!

121

Please bring...	**Παρακαλώ, φέρτε...**
	parakal**o** f**e**rte...
more bread	**κι άλλο ψωμί**
	kee **a**lo psom**ee**
more water	**κι άλλο νερό**
	kee **a**lo ner**o**
another bottle	**άλλο ένα μπουκάλι**
	alo **e**na book**a**lee
the bill	**το λογαριασμό**
	to loghareeasm**o**

Reading the menu

A Greek meal usually consists of one substantial main course, often with chips and salad, followed by a simple dessert such as fresh fruit. Bread is absolutely compulsory and Greeks often order a few side dishes to share.

Starters ΟΡΕΚΤΙΚΑ (orekteek**a**)

τζατζίκι (tzatz**ee**kee) yoghurt, cucumber, and garlic dip

ταραμοσαλάτα (taramosal**a**ta) dip made from fish roe

ελιές (ely**e**s) olives usually marinated in olive oil and garlic γιαούρτι (ya**oo**rtee) yogurt

καλαμάρια (kalam**a**rya) sliced squid in batter

κεφτέδες (keft**e**dhes) meat balls

αγγουροντομάτα (angoorondom**a**ta) tomato
   and cucumber salad

φέτα (f**e**ta) feta cheese

χταπόδι (khtap**o**dhee) octopus

λουκάνικο (look**a**neeko) sausage

Greek dishes you might like to try

ντολμαδάκια (dolmadh**a**kya) stuffed vineleaves

πιπεριές γεμιστές (peeper**ye**s yemeest**e**s) stuffed
   peppers

παστίτσιο (past**ee**tsyo) layers of pasta and
   minced meat, with a white sauce topping

μουσακάς (moossak**a**s) layers of aubergines and
   minced meat

γιουβέτσι (yoov**e**tsee) roast lamb with pasta

στιφάδο (steef**a**dho) beef and onions

Meat & poultry
ΚΡΕΑΣ ΚΑΙ ΠΟΥΛΕΡΙΚΑ (kr**e**as ke poolereek**a**)

μπριζόλα μοσχαρίσια (breez**o**la moskhar**ee**sya)
   beefsteak

μπριζόλα χοιρινή (breez**o**la kheereen**ee**)
   pork chop

σουβλάκι χοιρινό (soovlakee kheereeno)
pork kebab

σουβλάκι αρνίσιο (soovlakee arneesyo)
lamb kebab

παϊδάκια αρνίσια (paeedhakya arneesya)
lamb chops

μοσχάρι ψητό (moskharee pseeto) roast beef

κοτόπουλο ψητό (kotopoolo pseeto) roast chicken

Fish ΨΑΡΙΑ (psareea)

γαρίδες (ghareedhes) prawns

μπαρμπούνι (barboonee) red mullet

λιθρίνι (leethreenee) grey mullet

αστακός (astakos) lobster

ξιφίας (kseefeeas) swordfish

γλώσσα (ghlosa) sole

σουπιές (soopyes) cuttlefish

λαβράκι (lavrakee) sea bass

τσιπούρα (tseepoora) sea bream

Eggs ΑΒΓΑ (avgha)

αβγά τηγανητά (avgha teeghaneeta) fried eggs

αβγά βραστά (avgha vrasta) boiled eggs

ομελέτα (omeleta) omelette

αβγά ζαμπόν (avgha zambon) ham and eggs

Vegetables ΛΑΧΑΝΙΚΑ (lakhaneeka)

μπάμιες (bamyes) okra, 'lady's fingers'
σπανάκι (spanakee) spinach
κολοκυθάκια (kolokeethakya) courgettes
μελιτζάνες (meleetzanes) aubergines, eggplant
καρότα (karota) carrots
αγγούρι (angooree) cucumber
ντομάτα (domata) tomato
μαρούλι (maroolee) lettuce
πατάτες (patates) potatoes
πατάτες τηγανητές (patates teeghaneetes)
  fried potatoes
πατάτες πουρέ (patates poore) mashed potatoes
πατάτες φούρνου (patates foornoo)
  roast potatoes

Fruit ΦΡΟΥΤΑ (froota)

σταφύλια (stafeelya) grapes
καρπούζι (karpoozee) watermelon
πεπόνι (peponee) melon
σύκα (seeka) figs
αχλάδια (akhladhya) pears
μήλα (meela) apples
κεράσια (kerasya) cherries
ροδάκινα (rodhakeena) peaches
βερίκοκα (vereekoka) apricots
φράουλες (fraooles) strawberries
μπανάνες (bananes) bananas

Although you may find some of these in restaurants, a Greek meal is rarely followed by a sweet dessert; it is more usual to have fresh fruit. The place to go for Greek sweets is the patisserie, **ΖΑΧΑΡΟΠΛΑΣΤΕΙΟ** (zakharoplast**ee**o).

πάστες (p**a**stes) slices of gateaux
μπακλαβάς (baklav**a**s) filo pastry filled with chopped almonds, in syrup
κανταΐφι (kanda**ee**fee) shredded pastry with a filling of chopped almonds, in syrup
παγωτό (paghot**o**) ice cream
γαλατομπούρεκο (ghalatob**oo**reko) filo pastry with a cream filling, in syrup
κομπόστα (kob**o**sta) stewed or tinned fruit

Vegetarian

• •

You have to be a bit inventive! Although the Greeks
eat a large number of vegetarian dishes in their own
homes, they usually expect meat or fish when they
go out to eat. There are some specialist vegetarian
restaurants mainly catering for tourists.

Are there any vegetarian restaurants here?	**Υπάρχουν καθόλου εστιατόρια για χορτοφάγους εδώ;** eep**a**rkhoon kath**o**loo esteeat**o**reea ya khortof**a**ghoos edh**o**?
Do you have any vegetarian dishes?	**Έχετε καθόλου φαγητά για χορτοφάγους;** **e**khete kath**o**loo fa-yeet**a** ya khortof**a**ghoos?
Which dishes have no meat/ fish?	**Ποια φαγητά δεν έχουν κρέας/ψάρι;** pya fa-yeet**a** dhen **e**khoon kr**e**as/ps**a**ree?
What fish dishes do you have?	**Τι φαγητά με ψάρια έχετε;** tee fa-yeet**a** me ps**a**rya **e**khete?
I don't like meat	**Δεν μου αρέσει το κρέας** dhen moo ar**e**see to kr**e**as
What do you recommend?	**Τι προτείνετε;** tee prot**ee**nete?

Possible dishes

μπάμιες (b**a**myes) okra or 'ladies' fingers', usually cooked in a tomato sauce

γίγαντες (y**ee**gantes) large butter beans, usually in tomato sauce with olive oil and herbs

μελιτζάνες (meleetz**a**nes) aubergines, usually stuffed

χωριάτικη σαλάτα (khory**a**teekee sal**a**ta) village salad, usually containing tomatoes, cucumber, olives, onions, feta cheese and a dressing of olive oil and lemon or vinegar

γεμιστά (yemeest**a**) tomatoes and peppers stuffed with rice and herbs

φασολάκια (fasol**a**kya) green beans simmered in olive oil and tomato

φακές (fak**e**s) lentil soup

Wines and spirits

The wine list, please	**Τον κατάλογο των κρασιών, παρακαλώ**
	ton kat**a**logho ton krasy**o**n, parakal**o**
Can you recommend a good wine?	**Μπορείτε να μας προτείνετε ένα καλό κρασί;**
	bor**ee**te na mas prot**ee**nete **e**na kal**o** kras**ee**?
A bottle...	**Ένα μπουκάλι…**
	ena book**a**lee…
A carafe...	**Μία καράφα…**
	m**ee**a kar**a**fa…
of (house) wine	**κρασί**
	kras**ee**
of red wine	**κόκκινο κρασί**
	k**o**keeno kras**ee**
of white wine	**λευκό κρασί**
	lefk**o** kras**ee**
of rosé wine	**κρασί ροζέ**
	kras**ee** roz**e**
of dry wine	**ξηρό κρασί**
	kseer**o** kras**ee**
of sweet wine	**γλυκό κρασί**
	ghleek**o** kras**ee**
of a local wine	**τοπικό κρασί**
	topeek**o** kras**ee**

Wines

Χατζημιχάλη (khadzeemeekhalee) a range of wines from N. Greece

Αχαία Κλάους (akhaya klaoos) a range of wines from the Peloponnese

Ζίτσα (zeetsa) sparkling white wine from Epirus

Αβέρωφ (averof) red wines from Epirus

Απέλια (apeleea) dry white wine

Δεμέστιχα (dhemesteekha) a dry wine, white or red

Κιτρό (keetro) a slightly sour white wine from Naxos

Κοκκινέλι (kokeenelee) a sweet red wine from Crete

Τσάνταλη (tsantalee) a selection of wines from Thrace and Macedonia

Αγιορείτικο (ayoreeteeko) wine made by monks on Mt Athos

Μάντικο (manteeko) a dry red wine from Crete

Μαυροδάφνη (mavrodhafnee) a sweet red dessert wine

Μόντε Χρήστος (monte khreestos) a sweet red wine from Cyprus

Μοσχάτο (moskhato) dark red dessert wine with muscatel flavour

Αφροδίτη (afrodheetee) a medium white wine from Cyprus

Ροδάμπελη (rodhabelee) a dry white wine

Σάμος (samos) traditional wine from the Aegean island of Samos

Νεμέας (nem**e**as) dry red wine from Nemea, Peloponnese

Beers

Beer is of the lager type and both bottled beer and draught are available. Some is brewed in Greece, some imported.

Spirits

κονιάκ (kony**a**k) brandy, ranked by a star system: the more stars, the better quality the brandy
ούζο (**oo**zo) an aniseed-flavoured colourless drink, drunk on its own or with water. When water is added it turns white
ρακή (rak**ee**) a clear strong spirit

Other drinks to try

ρετσίνα (rets**ee**na) a resinated white wine which can accompany a meal but can equally well be enjoyed on its own, especially well chilled or with soda, lemonade or Coke
κουμανταρία (koomantar**ee**a) very sweet dessert wine from Cyprus
φιλφάρ (feelf**a**r) an orange-flavoured liqueur from Cyprus

Menu reader

α A

αγγούρι ang**oo**ree cucumber

αγκινάρες ankeen**a**res artichokes

αεριούχο aeree**oo**kho fizzy, sparkling

αθερίνα ather**ee**na whitebait, usually fried

αλάτι al**a**tee salt

αλεύρι al**e**vree flour

αμύγδαλα am**ee**ghdhala almonds

αρακάς arak**a**s peas

αρνί arn**ee** lamb

αρνί γιουβέτσι arn**ee** yoov**e**tsee roast lamb with small pasta

αρνί λεμονάτο arn**ee** lemon**a**to lamb braised in sauce with herbs and lemon juice

αρνί ψητό arn**ee** pseet**o** roast lamb

αστακός astak**o**s lobster (often served with lemon juice and olive oil)

άσπρο **a**spro white

άσπρο κρασί **a**spro kras**ee** white wine

αυγά avgh**a** eggs

αυγολέμονο avghol**e**mono egg and lemon soup

αφέλια af**e**leea pork in red wine with seasonings

αχλάδι akhl**a**dhee pear

β B

βερίκοκο ver**ee**koko apricot

βλίτα vl**ee**ta wild greens (like spinach, eaten with olive oil and lemon)

βοδινό vodheen**o** beef

βουτήματα voot**ee**mata biscuits to dip in coffee

βούτυρο v**oo**teero butter

βραδινό vradeen**o** evening meal

βραστό vrast**o** boiled

γ Γ

γάλα gh**a**la milk

γαλακτομπούρικο ghalaktob**oo**reeko custard tart

γαρίδες ghar**ee**dhes shrimps; prawns

γαύρος gavros sardine-type fish (if salted: anchovy)

γίδα βραστή y**ee**da vrast**ee** goat soup

γεμιστά yemeest**a** stuffed vegetables

γιαούρτι ya**oo**rtee yoghurt

γιαούρτι με μέλι ya**oo**rtee me m**e**lee yoghurt with honey

γιαχνί yakhn**ee** cooked in tomato sauce and olive oil

γίγαντες y**ee**ghantes large butter beans

γιουβαρελάκια yoovarel**a**kya meatballs in lemon sauce

γλυκά ghleek**a** desserts

γλυκά κουταλιού ghleek**a** kootaly**oo** crystallized fruits in syrup

γλώσσα ghl**o**sa sole

γόπες gh**o**pes bogue, a type of fish

133

γραβιέρα ghravyera cheese resembling gruyère
γύρος yeeros doner kebab

δ Δ
δείπνο dheepno dinner
δίπλες dheeples pastry with honey and walnuts

ε Ε
ελάχιστα ψημένο elakheesta pseemeno rare (meat)
ελαιόλαδο eleoladho olive oil
ελιές elyes olives
ελιές τσακιστές elyes tsakeestes cracked green
  olives with coriander seeds and garlic (Cyprus)
εξοχικό eksokheeko stuffed pork or beef with
  vegetables and cheese

ζ Ζ
ζαμπόν zambon ham
ζάχαρη zakharee sugar
ζεστή σοκολάτα zestee sokolata hot chocolate
ζεστό zesto hot, warm

θ Θ
Θαλασσινά thalaseena seafood
Θυμάρι theemaree thyme

ι Ι
ιμάμ μπαϊλντί eemam baeeldee stuffed
  aubergines (eggplants)

κ K

κάβα kava wine shop

καγιανάς με παστό κρέας kayan**a**s me past**o** kr**e**as salted pork with cheese, tomatoes and eggs

κακαβιά kakavy**a** fish soup

κακάο kak**ow** hot chocolate

καλαμάκι kalam**a**kee straw (for drinking); small skewer

καλαμάρια kalam**a**rya squid

καλοψημένο kalopseem**e**no well done (meat)

κανέλα kan**e**lla cinnamon

κάπαρι k**a**paree pickled capers

καπνιστό kapneest**o** smoked

καπουτσίνο kapoots**ee**no cappucino

καράφα kar**a**fa carafe

καρότο kar**o**to carrot

καρπούζι karp**oo**zee watermelon

καρύδι kar**ee**dhee walnut

καρυδόπιτα kareedh**o**peeta walnut cake

κασέρι kas**e**ree type of cheese

κάστανα k**a**stana chestnuts

καταΐφι kata**ee**fee small shredded pastry drenched in syrup

κατάλογος kat**a**loghos menu

κατάλογος κρασιών kat**a**loghos krasy**o**n wine list

καταψυγμένο katapseeghm**e**no frozen

κατσίκι kats**ee**kee roast kid

καφενείο kafen**ee**o café

καφές kaf**e**s coffee (Greek-style)

καφέδες kaf**e**dhes coffees (plural)

καφές γλυκύς kaf**e**s ghleek**ee**s very sweet coffee

καφές μέτριος kaf**e**s m**e**treeos medium-sweet coffee

καφές σκέτος kaf**e**s sk**e**tos coffee without sugar

κεράσια ker**a**sya cherries

κεφαλοτύρι kefalot**ee**ree type of cheese, often served fried in olive oil

κεφτέδες keft**e**dhes meat balls

κιμάς keem**a**s mince

κλέφτικο kl**e**fteeko casserole with lamb, potatoes and vegetables

κοκορέτσι kokor**e**tsee traditional spit-roasted dish of spiced liver and other offal

κολοκυθάκια kolokeeth**a**kya courgettes, zucchini

κολοκυθόπιτα kolokeeth**o**peeta courgette/zucchini pie

κονιάκ kony**a**k brandy, cognac

κοντοσούβλι kontos**oo**vlee spicy pieces of lamb, pork or beef, spit-roasted

κοτόπουλο kot**o**poolo chicken

κουλούρια kool**oo**rya bread rings

κουνέλι koon**e**lee rabbit

κουνουπίδι koonoop**ee**dhee cauliflower

κουπέπια koop**e**pya stuffed vine leaves (Cyprus)

κουπές koop**e**s meat pasties

κουραμπιέδες koorambyi**e**dhes small almond cakes eaten at Christmas

κρασί kras**ee** wine

κρέας kreas meat

κρέμα krema cream

κρεμμύδια kremeedhya onions

κρητική σαλάτα kreeteekee salata watercress salad

κρύο kreeo cold

κυνήγι keeneeghee game

κύριο πιάτο keereeo pyato main course

λ Λ

λαγός laghos hare

λάδι ladhee oil

λαδότυρο ladhoteero soft cheese with olive oil

λάχανα lakhana green vegetables

λαχανικά lakhaneeka vegetables (menu heading)

λάχανο lakhano cabbage, greens

λεμονάδα lemonadha lemon drink

λεμόνι lemonee lemon

λευκό lefko white (used for wine as well as **άσπρο**)

λίγο leegho a little, a bit

λουκάνικα lookaneeka type of highly seasoned
  sausage

λουκουμάδες lookoomadhes small fried dough
  balls in syrup

λουκούμι lookoomee Turkish delight

λούντζα loondza loin of pork, marinated and smoked

μ Μ

μαγειρίτσα mayeereetsa soup made of lamb offal,
  special Easter dish

μαϊντανός maeedan**o**s parsley

μακαρόνια makar**o**nya spaghetti

μακαρόνια με κιμά makar**o**nya me keem**a** spaghetti bolognese

μαρίδες mar**ee**dhes small fish like sprats, served fried

μαρούλι mar**oo**lee lettuce

μαύρο κρασί m**a**vro kras**ee** red wine (although you'll hear k**o**keeno kras**ee** more often)

μανιτάρια maneet**a**rya mushrooms

μαυρομάτικα mavrom**a**teeka black-eyed peas

μεγάλο megh**a**lo large, big

μεζές mez**e**s (plural **μεζέδες** mez**e**dhes) small snacks served free of charge with ouzo or retsina; assortment of mini-portions of various dishes, available on the menu (or on request) at some restaurants

μεζεδοπωλείο mezedhopol**ee**o taverna/shop selling **mezedhes**

μέλι m**e**lee honey

μελιτζάνα meleetz**a**na aubergine (eggplant)

μελιτζάνες ιμάμ meleetz**a**nes eem**a**m aubergines (eggplants) stuffed with tomato and onion

μελιτζανοσαλάτα meleetzanos**a**lata aubergine (eggplant) mousse (dip)

μεσημεριανό meseemeryan**o** lunch

μεταλλικό νερό metale**e**ko ner**o** mineral water

μεταξά metaks**a** Metaxa (Greek brandy-type spirit)

μέτρια ψημένο metreea pseemeno medium-grilled (meat)

μη αεριούχο mee aereeookho still, not fizzy

μήλα meela apples

μηλόπιτα meelopeeta apple pie

μοσχάρι moskharee beef

μοσχάρι κοκινιστό moskharee kokeeneesto beef in wine sauce with tomatoes and onions

μουσακάς moosakas moussaka, layers of aubergine (eggplant), minced meat and potato, with white sauce

μπακαλιάρος bakalyaros cod

μπακαλιάρος παστός bakalyaros pastos salt cod

μπακλαβάς baklavas filo-pastry with nuts soaked in syrup

μπάμιες bamyes okra, ladies' fingers (vegetable)

μπαρμπούνι barboonee red mullet

μπέικον be-eekon bacon

μπιφτέκι beeftekee beef rissole/burger

μπουγάτσα booghatsa cheese or custard pastry sprinkled with sugar and cinnamon

μπουρέκι boorekee cheese, potato and courgette pie

μπουρέκια boorekya puff pastry filled with meat and cheese (Cyprus)

μπριάμ(ι) breeam(ee) ratatouille

μπριζόλα breezola steak/chop

μπριζόλα αρνίσια breezola arneesya lamb chop

μπριζόλα μοσχαρίσια breezola moskhareesya beef steak/chop

μπριζόλα χοιρινή breez**o**la kheereen**ee** pork chop
μπύρα b**ee**ra beer
μύδια m**ee**dhya mussels

ν N

νες, νεσκαφέ nes, nescaf**e** instant coffee (of any
  brand)
  νες με γάλα nes me gh**a**la coffee (instant) with milk
  νες φραπέ nes frapp**e** iced coffee
νερό ner**o** water
ντολμάδες dolm**a**dhes vine leaves, rolled up and
  stuffed with rice and sometimes mince
ντομάτες dom**a**tes tomatoes
ντομάτες γεμιστές dom**a**tes yemeest**es** tomatoes
  stuffed with rice and herbs, and sometimes with
  mince

ξ Ξ

ξιφίας kseef**ee**as swordfish
ξύδι ks**ee**dhee vinegar

ο Ο

ομελέτα omel**e**tta omelette
ορεκτικά orekteek**a** first courses/starters (menu
  heading)
ουζερί oozer**ee** small bar selling ouzo and other
  drinks, maybe with **mezedhes** (μεζέδες)
ούζο **oo**zo ouzo (traditional aniseed-flavoured spirit)
οχταπόδι okhtap**o**dhee octopus (see also **χταπόδι**)

οχταπόδι κρασάτο okhtap**o**dhee krasato octopus in red wine sauce

π Π

παγάκια pagh**a**kya ice-cubes

παγωτό paghot**o** ice-cream

παϊδάκια paeedh**a**kya grilled lamb chops

παντζάρια pandz**a**rya beetroot with seasonings

παξιμάδια pakseem**a**dhya crispy bread (baked twice)

παπουτσάκια papoots**a**kya stuffed aubergines (eggplants)

πάστα p**a**sta cake, pastry

παστό past**o** salted

παστιτσάδα pasteets**a**da beef with tomatoes, onions, red wine, herbs, spices and pasta

παστίτσιο past**ee**tseeo baked pasta dish with a middle layer of meat and white sauce

πατσάς pats**a**s tripe soup

πατάτες pat**a**tes potatoes

πατάτες τηγανιτές pat**a**tes teeghaneet**e**s chips, fries

πεπόνι pep**o**nee melon

πιάτο της ημέρας p**ya**to tees eem**e**ras dish of the day

πιλάφι peel**a**fee rice

πιπέρι peep**e**ree pepper

πιπεριές peepery**e**s peppers

πιπεριές γεμιστές peepery**e**s yemeest**e**s stuffed peppers with rice, herbs and sometimes mince

πίτα or **πίττα** p**ee**ta pitta (flat unleavened bread);
pie with different fillings, such as meat, cheese,
vegetables

πλακί plak**ee** fish in tomato sauce

πορτοκαλάδα portokal**a**dha orangeade

πορτοκάλια portok**a**lya oranges

πουργούρι poorgh**oo**ree cracked wheat (Cyprus)

πουργούρι πιλάφι poorgh**oo**ree peel**a**fee salad
made of cracked wheat (Cyprus)

πρωινό proeen**o** breakfast

ρ P

ραβιόλι ravy**o**lee pastry stuffed with cheese (Cyprus)

ραδίκια radh**ee**kya chicory

ρακή, ρακί rak**ee** raki, strong spirit a bit like
schnapps

ρεβίθια rev**ee**thya chickpeas

ρέγγα r**e**nga herring

ρέγγα καπνιστή r**e**nga kapneest**ee** smoked
herring, kipper

ρετσίνα rets**ee**na retsina, traditional resinated
white wine

ρίγανη r**ee**ghanee oregano

ροδάκινο rodh**a**keeno peach

ροζέ κρασί roz**e** kras**ee** rosé wine

ρύζι r**ee**zee rice

ρυζόγαλο reez**o**ghalo rice pudding

σ ς Σ

σαγανάκι saghan**a**kee cheese coated in flour and fried in olive oil

σαλάτα sal**a**ta salad

σαλιγκάρια saleeng**a**rya snails

σαρδέλλες sardh**e**les sardines

σέλινο s**e**leeno celery, celeriac

σεφταλιά seftaly**a** minced pork pasty

σικαλένιο ψωμί seekal**e**nyo psom**ee** rye bread

σικώτι seek**o**tee liver

σκορδαλιά skordhaly**a** garlic and potato mash

σκορδαλιά με ψάρι τηγανιτό skordhaly**a** me ps**a**ree teeghaneet**o** fried fish served with garlic and potato mash

σκόρδο sk**o**rdho garlic

σόδα s**o**dha soda

σουβλάκι soovl**a**kee meat kebab

σουβλατζίδικο soovlats**ee**deeko shop selling souvlakia, doner kebabs, etc

σούπα s**oo**pa soup

σουπιά soopy**a** cuttlefish

σουτζουκάκια sootzook**a**kya highly seasoned meat balls

σπανάκι span**a**kee spinach

σπανακόπιτα spanak**o**peeta spinach pie

σπαράγγια σαλάτα spar**a**ngya sal**a**ta asparagus salad

σταφύλια staf**ee**lya grapes

στη σούβλα stee s**oo**vla spit-roasted

στιφάδο steef**a**dho braised beef in spicy onion and tomato sauce

στο φούρνο sto f**oo**rno baked in the oven

στρείδια str**ee**dhya oysters

σύκα s**ee**ka figs

σχάρας skh**a**ras grilled

τ Τ

ταραμοσαλάτα taramosal**a**ta mousse of cod roe

τζατζίκι tzatz**ee**kee yoghurt, garlic and cucumber dip

τηγανιτό teeghaneet**o** fried

τραπανός trapan**o**s soup made of cracked wheat and yoghurt (Cyprus)

τραπέζι trap**e**zee table

τσάι ts**a**ee tea

τσιπούρα tseep**oo**ra type of sea bream

τσουρέκι tsoor**e**kee festive bread

τυρί teer**ee** cheese

τυροκαυτερή teerokafter**ee** spicy dip made of cheese and peppers

τυρόπιτα teer**o**peeta cheese pie

τυροσαλάτα teerosal**a**ta starter made of cream cheese and herbs

φ Φ

φάβα f**a**va yellow split peas or lentils, served in a purée with olive oil and capers

φακές fak**e**s lentils

φασολάδα fasol**a**dha soup made with white beans
and vegetables, eaten with lemon

φασολάκια fasol**a**kya green beans

φασόλια fas**o**lya haricot beans

φέτα f**e**ta feta cheese, tangy white cheese used in
salads and other dishes; a slice

φλαούνες fla**oo**nes Easter cheese cake (Cyprus)

φράουλες fr**a**ooles strawberries

φραπέ frapp**e** iced coffee

φρέσκο fr**e**sko fresh

φυστίκια Αιγίνης feest**ee**kya egh**ee**nees pistacchios

χ X

χαλβάς khalv**a**s sesame seed sweet

χαλούμι khal**oo**mee ewe's- or goat's-milk cheese,
often grilled

χοιρινό kheereen**o** pork

χόρτα kh**o**rta wild greens (similar to spinach) eaten
cold with oil and lemon

χορτοφάγος khortof**a**ghos vegetarian

χούμους kh**oo**moos dip made with puréed
chickpeas, hummus (Cyprus)

χταπόδι khtap**o**dhee octopus, grilled or as a
side-salad

χωριάτικη σαλάτα khory**a**teekee sal**a**ta salad,
Greek-style, with tomatoes, feta cheese,
cucumber, onions, olives and oregano

ψ æ

ψάρι ps**a**ree fish

ψάρια καπνιστά ps**a**rya kapneest**a** smoked fish

ψάρια πλακί ps**a**rya plak**ee** baked whole fish with vegetables and tomatoes

ψαρόσουπα psar**o**soopa seafood soup

ψαροταβέρνα psarotav**e**rna fish taverna

ψησταριά pseestary**a** grill house

ψητό pseet**o** roast/grilled

ψωμί psom**ee** bread

ψωμί ολικής αλέσεως psom**ee** oleek**ee**s al**e**seos wholemeal bread

Phonetic menu reader

••

aeree**oo**kho fizzy, sparkling

af**e**leea pork in red wine with seasonings (Cyprus)

aghreeogh**oo**roono wild boar

akheen**ee** sea urchin roes

akhl**a**dhee pear

akhl**a**dhee sto f**oo**rno baked pear in syrup sauce

akhneest**o** steamed

al**a**tee salt

al**e**vree flour

alevr**o**peeta pie made with cheese, milk and eggs

am**ee**ghdhala almonds

aneethos dill

ang**oo**ree cucumber

ankeen**a**res **a**la pol**ee**ta artichokes with lemon juice
and olive oil

ankeen**a**res artichokes

arak**a**s peas

arn**ee** lamb

arn**ee** lemon**a**to lamb braised in sauce with herbs
and lemon juice

arn**ee** me v**o**tana lamb braised with vegetables and
herbs

arn**ee** pseet**o** roast lamb

arn**ee** yoov**e**tsee roast lamb with small pasta

arn**ee**see-es breez**o**les lamb chops

aspro kras**ee** white wine

147

aspro white

astak**o**s lobster (often served with lemon juice and olive oil)

ather**ee**na whitebait, usually fried

avgh**a** eggs

avghol**e**mono egg and lemon soup

avghot**a**rakho mullet roe (smoked)

bakalee**a**ros cod

bakalee**a**ros past**o**s salt cod

baklav**a**s filo-pastry with nuts soaked in syrup

b**a**meeyes okra, ladies' fingers (vegetable)

bar**a**kee bar

barb**oo**nee red mullet

be-**e**ekon bacon

beeft**e**kee beef rissole/burger

b**ee**ra beer

boogh**a**tsa cheese or custard pastry sprinkled with sugar and cinnamon

book**a**lee bottle

boordh**e**to fish or meat in a thick sauce of onions, tomatoes and red peppers

boor**e**kee cheese potato, and courgette pie

boor**e**keea puff pastry filled with meat and cheese (Cyprus)

bree**a**m(ee) ratatouille

breez**o**la steak/chop

breez**o**la arn**ee**sya lamb chop

breez**o**la kheereen**ee** pork chop
breez**o**la moskhar**ee**sya beef steak/chop

dendrol**ee**vano rosemary
dh**a**fnee bay leaf
dh**a**kteela almond cakes
dham**a**skeena plums, prunes
dh**ee**ples pastry with honey and walnuts
dh**ee**pno dinner
dholm**a**dhes vine leaves, rolled up and stuffed with
   minced meat and rice
dolm**a**dhes vine leaves, rolled up and stuffed with rice
   and sometimes mince
dom**a**tes tomatoes
dom**a**tes yemeest**e**s tomatoes stuffed with rice and
   herbs, and sometimes with mince

eem**a**m baeeld**ee** stuffed aubergines (eggplants)
eenopol**ee**o wine shop
eksokheek**o** stuffed pork or beef with vegetables
   and cheese
el**a**kheesta pseem**e**no rare (meat)
ele**o**ladho olive oil
ely**e**s olives
ely**e**s tsakeest**e**s cracked green olives with coriander
   seeds and garlic (Cyprus)
elyot**ee** olive bread
esteeat**o**reeo restaurant

fak**e**s lentils
fangr**ee** sea bream
fasol**a**dha soup made with white beans and
  vegetables, eaten with lemon
fasol**a**keea green beans
fas**o**leea haricot beans
f**a**va yellow split peas or lentils, served in a purée
  with olive oil and capers
feest**ee**kya peanuts
feest**ee**kya egh**ee**nees pistacchios
f**e**ta feta cheese, tangy white cheese used in salads
  and other dishes; a slice
fla**oo**nes Easter cheese cake (Cyprus)
fr**a**ooles strawberries
frapp**e** iced coffee
fr**e**sko fresh

g**a**vros sardine-type fish (if salted: anchovy)
gh**a**la milk
ghalaktob**oo**reeko custard tart
ghalaktopol**ee**o café/patisserie
ghar**ee**dhes shrimps; prawns
ghar**ee**dhes yoov**e**tsee prawns in tomato sauce
  with feta
ghar**ee**falo clove (spice)
ghaz**o**za fizzy drink
ghleek**a** desserts
ghleek**a** kootaly**oo** crystallized fruits in syrup

ghl**o**sa sole
gh**o**pes bogue, a type of fish
ghravy**e**ra cheese resembling gruyère
kaf**e**dhes coffees (plural)
kafen**ee**o café
kaf**e**s coffee (Greek-style)
kaf**e**s ghleek**ee**s very sweet coffee
kaf**e**s m**e**treeos medium-sweet coffee
kaf**e**s sk**e**tos coffee without sugar
kakavee**a** fish soup
kak**o**w hot chocolate
kalam**a**kee straw (for drinking); small skewer
kalam**a**reea squid
kalam**a**reea teeghaneet**a** fried squid
kalamb**o**kee corn on the cob
kalambok**o**peeta corn bread
kalopseem**e**no well done (meat)
kan**e**lla cinnamon
k**a**paree pickled capers
kapneest**o** smoked
kapoots**ee**no cappucino
kar**a**fa carafe
karav**ee**dha crayfish
kar**ee**dha coconut
kar**ee**dhee walnut
kareedh**o**peeta walnut cake
kar**e**kla chair
kar**o**to carrot

karp**oo**zee watermelon

kas**e**ree type of cheese

k**a**stana chestnuts

kata**ee**fee small shredded pastry drenched in syrup

kat**a**loghos menu

kat**a**loghos krasy**o**n wine list

katapseeghm**e**no frozen

kats**ee**kee roast kid

k**a**va wine shop

k**a**vooras boiled crab

kayan**a**s me past**o** kr**e**yas salted pork with cheese, tomatoes and eggs

keedh**o**nee quince

keedh**o**nee sto f**oo**rno baked quince

keedh**o**neea type of clams, cockles

keem**a**s mince

keen**ee**ghee game

k**ee**reeo py**a**to main course

kefalot**ee**ree type of cheese, often served fried in olive oil

keft**e**dhes meat balls

ker**a**seea cherries

khal**oo**mee ewe's- or goat's-milk cheese, often grilled

khalv**a**s sesame seed sweet

kheereen**o** pork

kheereen**o** kreet**ee**k**o** baked pork chops (Crete)

kheerom**e**ree marinated, smoked ham

kh**e**lee kapneest**o** smoked eel

kh**oo**moos dip made with puréed chickpeas, hummus (Cyprus)

khoree**a**teekee sal**a**ta salad, Greek-style, with tomatoes, feta cheese, cucumber, onions, olives and oregano

kh**o**rta wild greens (similar to spinich) eaten cold with oil and lemon

khortof**a**ghos vegetarian

khtap**o**dhee octopus, grilled or as a side-salad

kl**e**fteeko casserole with lamb, potatoes and vegetables

kokor**e**tsee traditional spit-roasted dish of spiced liver and other offal

kokt**e**-**ee**l cocktail

kolatsy**o** brunch, elevenses

kolokeeth**a**keea courgettes, zucchini

kolokeeth**o**peeta courgette/zucchini pie

kolokeeth**o**peeta gleeky**a** sweet courgette/zucchini pie

kolok**o**tes pastries with pumpkin seeds and raisins

kontos**oo**vlee spicy pieces of lamb, pork or beef, spit-roasted

kony**a**k brandy, cognac

kooky**a** broad beans

kool**oo**reea bread rings

koon**e**lee rabbit

koonoop**ee**dhee cauliflower

koop**e**peea stuffed vine leaves (Cyprus)

koop**e**s meat pasties
kooramby**e**dhes small almond cakes eaten at
   Christmas
kot**o**poolo chicken
kot**o**poolo kapam**a** chicken casseroled with red
   peppers, onions, cinnamon and raisins
kot**o**poolo reeghan**a**to grilled basted chicken
   with herbs
kras**ee** wine
kr**e**as meat
kr**ee**o cold
kreeteek**ee** sal**a**ta watercress salad
kr**e**ma cream
krem**ee**dheea onions
ks**ee**dhee vinegar
kseef**ee**as swordfish

l**a**dhee oil
ladher**a** vegetable casserole
ladh**o**teero soft cheese with olive oil
lagh**o**s hare
l**a**khana green vegetables
lakhaneek**a** vegetables (menu heading)
l**a**khano cabbage, greens
lavr**a**kee sea-bass
l**ee**gho a little, a bit
lefk**o** white
lemon**a**dha lemon drink

lem**o**nee lemon
look**a**neeka type of highly seasoned sausage
lookoom**a**dhes small fried dough balls in syrup
look**oo**mee Turkish delight
look**oo**meea shortbread served at weddings
l**oo**ndza loin of pork, marinated and smoked

maeedan**o**s parsley
makar**o**nya spaghetti
makar**o**nya me keem**a** spaghetti bolognese
maneet**a**reea mushrooms
mar**ee**dhes small fish like sprats, served fried
mar**oo**lee lettuce
mart**ee**nee martini
m**a**vro kras**ee** red wine (although you'll hear k**o**keeno
  kras**ee** more often)
mavrom**a**teeka black-eyed peas
mayeer**ee**tsa soup made of lamb offal, special
  Easter dish
mee aeree**oo**kho still, not fizzy
m**ee**dheea mussels
meekr**o** small, little
m**ee**la apples
m**ee**lko chocolate milk
meelks**e**ik milkshake
meel**o**peeta apple pie
megh**a**lo large, big
m**e**lee honey

meleetz**a**na aubergine (eggplant)

meleetzan**a**kee gleek**o** crystallized sweet in syrup, made from aubergine/eggplant

meleetz**a**nes eem**a**m aubergines (eggplants) stuffed with tomato and onion

meleetzanosal**a**ta aubergine (eggplant) mousse (dip)

meseemeree**a**no lunch

metaks**a** Metaxa (Greek brandy-type spirit)

metaleek**o** ner**o** mineral water

m**e**treea pseem**e**no medium-grilled (meat)

mezedhopol**ee**o taverna/shop selling mezedhes

mez**e**s (plural **μεζέδες** mez**e**dhes) small snacks served free of charge with ouzo or retsina; assortment of mini-portions of various dishes, available on the menu (or on request) at some restaurants.

moosak**a**s moussaka, layers of aubergine (eggplant), minced meat and potato, with white sauce

moskh**a**ree beef

moskh**a**ree kokeeneest**o** beef in wine sauce with tomatoes and onions

ner**o** water

nes frapp**e** iced coffee

nes me gh**a**la coffee (instant) with milk

nes, nescaf**e** instant coffee (of any brand)

okhtap**o**dhee octopus (see also **χταπόδι**)

okhtap**o**dhee kras**a**to octopus in red wine sauce

omel**e**tta omelette

oozeree small bar selling ouzo
and other drinks, maybe with mezedhes

oozo ouzo (traditional aniseed-flavoured spirit)

orekteek**a** first courses/starters (menu heading)

oveleest**ee**reeo shop selling souvlakia and doner
kebabs

paeedh**a**keea grilled lamb chops

pagh**a**kya ice-cubes

paghot**o** ice-cream

pakseem**a**dheea crispy bread (baked twice)

pakseemadhok**oo**loora tomato and cheese bread

pandz**a**reea beetroot with seasonings

papoots**a**keea stuffed aubergines (eggplants)

pasat**e**mpo pumpkin seeds

p**a**sta cake, pastry

pasteets**a**da beef with tomatoes, onions, red wine,
herbs, spices and pasta

past**ee**tseeo baked pasta dish with a middle layer of
meat and white sauce

past**o** salted

pat**a**tes potatoes

pat**a**tes teeghaneet**e**s chips, fries

pats**a**s tripe soup

peek**a**nteeko spicy

peel**a**fee rice

peeleeor**ee**teeko boob**a**ree spicy sausage

peep**e**ree pepper

peepery**e**s peppers

peepery**e**s yemeest**e**s stuffed peppers with rice,
   herbs and sometimes mince

p**ee**ta pitta (flat unleavened bread); pie with
   different fillings, such as meat, cheese, vegetables

pep**o**nee melon

p**e**strofa trout

plak**ee** fish in tomato sauce

poorgh**oo**ree cracked wheat (Cyprus)

poorgh**oo**ree peel**a**fee salad made of cracked wheat
   (Cyprus)

portokal**a**dha orangeade

portok**a**lya oranges

pr**a**sa me sees**a**mee leeks baked and sprinkled with
   sesame seeds

proeen**o** breakfast

ps**a**ree fish

ps**a**reea kapneest**a** smoked fish

ps**a**reea plak**ee** baked whole fish with vegetables
   and tomatoes

psar**o**soopa seafood soup

psarotav**e**rna fish taverna

pseestar**ee**a grill house

pseet**o** roast/grilled

psom**a**kee bread roll, bread bun

psom**ee** bread

psom**ee** oleek**ee**s al**e**seos wholemeal bread

py**a**to tees eem**e**ras dish of the day

radh**ee**keea chicory

rak**ee** raki, strong spirit a bit like schnapps

ravee**o**lee pastry stuffed with cheese (Cyprus)

r**ee**ghanee oregano

r**ee**zee rice

reez**o**ghalo rice pudding

r**e**nga herring

r**e**nga kapneest**ee** smoked herring, kipper

rets**ee**na retsina, traditional resinated white wine

rev**ee**theea chickpeas

rodh**a**keeno peach

rol**o** me keem**a** meatloaf

r**o**seekee sal**a**ta Russian salad (pieces of egg,
    potatoes, gherkins, peas and carrots in
    mayonnaise)

roz**e** kras**ee** rosé wine

saghan**a**kee cheese coated in flour and fried in
    olive oil

sal**a**khee ray

sal**a**ta salad

salateek**a** salads (menu heading)

saleeng**a**reea snails

saleeng**a**reea yakhn**ee** snails in tomato sauce

s**a**ndweets sandwich (sometimes a filled roll,
    sometimes a toasted sandwich with your own
    chosen combination of fillings)

sarangh**lee** pastry with walnuts, sesame seeds
    and syrup; sometimes chocolate too

sardh**e**les sardines

s**ee**ka figs

s**ee**ka sto f**oo**rno me mavrod**a**fnee figs cooked in
red wine sauce with spices

seekal**e**nyo psom**ee** rye bread

seek**o**tee liver

seftaly**a** minced pork pasty

s**e**leeno celery, celeriac

skh**a**ras grilled

skordhaly**a** garlic and potato mash

skordhaly**a** me ps**a**ree teeghaneet**o** fried fish served
with garlic and potato mash

sk**o**rdho garlic

s**o**dha soda

sofr**ee**to beef stew with creamy garlic sauce (Corfu)

s**oo**pa soup

soopy**a** cuttlefish

sootzook**a**kya highly seasoned meat balls

soovl**a**kee meat kebab

soovlats**ee**deeko shop selling souvlakia, doner
kebabs, etc

span**a**kee spinach

spanak**o**peeta spinach pie

spar**a**ngee asparagus

spar**a**ngya ke angeen**a**res asparagus and artichokes
with lemon

spar**a**ngya sal**a**ta asparagus salad

staf**ee**lya grapes

stee s**oo**vla spit-roasted

stee**fa**dho braised beef in spicy onion and tomato sauce

sto f**oo**rno baked in the oven

str**ee**dhya oysters

takh**ee**nee sesame seed paste

taramosal**a**ta mousse of cod roe

teeghaneet**o** fried

teer**ee** cheese

teerokafter**ee** spicy dip made of cheese and peppers

teer**o**peeta cheese pie

teerosal**a**ta starter made of cream cheese and herbs

thalaseen**a** seafood

theem**a**ree thyme

t**o**nos pseet**o**s grilled tuna with vegetables

trapan**o**s soup made of cracked wheat and yoghurt (Cyprus)

trap**e**zee table

ts**a**ee tea

tseep**oo**ra type of sea bream

tsoor**e**kee festive bread

tzatz**ee**kee yoghurt, garlic and cucumber dip

vaseeleek**o**s basil

veeseen**o** kas**e**ree sheep's cheese served with cherry preserve

ver**ee**koko apricot

vl**ee**ta wild greens (like spinach, eaten with olive oil and lemon)

vodheen**o** beef
voot**ee**mata biscuits to dip in coffee
v**oo**teero butter
v**o**tka vodka
vradeen**o** evening meal
vrast**o** boiled

weeskee whisky
yakhn**ee** cooked in tomato sauce and olive oil
ya**oo**rtee yoghurt
ya**oo**rtee me m**e**lee yoghurt with honey
y**ee**da vrast**ee** goat soup
y**ee**ghantes large butter beans
y**ee**ros doner kebab
yemeest**a** stuffed vegetables
yoovarl**a**kya meatballs in lemon sauce

z**a**kharee sugar
zakharoplast**ee**o cake shop
zamb**o**n ham
zelat**ee**na brawn
zest**ee** sokol**a**ta hot chocolate
zest**o** hot, warm

Grammar

The following basic rules of Greek grammar will help you make full use of the information in this book. Greek grammar is rather complicated by the fact that pronouns, nouns and adjectives change their endings according to their function in the sentence, their number (whether they are singular or plural) and their gender (whether they are masculine, feminine or neuter) – rather like German. A brief outline of the grammar is given here, but for a fuller explanation you should consult a Greek grammar book.

Nouns

A noun is a word used to refer to a person or thing, e.g. 'car', 'horse', 'Mary'. Greek nouns can be masculine, feminine or neuter, and the words for 'the' and 'a' (the articles) change according to the gender of the noun.

o (o)	= the with masculine nouns
η (ee)	= the with feminine nouns

το (to)	= the with neuter nouns
ένας (**e**nas)	= a with masculine nouns
μία (m**ee**a)	= a with feminine nouns
ένα (**e**na)	= a with neuter nouns

The article is the most reliable indication of the gender of a noun, i.e. whether it is masculine, feminine or neuter.

In the dictionary sections you will come across examples like this: **ο/η γιατρός** (yatr**o**s) doctor. This means that the same ending is used for men as well as women doctors i.e. **ο γιατρός** is a male doctor, **η γιατρός** is a female doctor.

You will also encounter entries like **ο Άγγλος/η Αγγλίδα** indicating that an Englishman is referred to as **ο Άγγλος** (**a**nglos) while an Englishwoman is **η Αγγλίδα** (angl**ee**dha).

Masculine endings of nouns

The most common endings of masculine nouns are **–ος** (os), **–ας** (as), **–ης** (ees), e.g.

ο καιρός (ker**o**s)	weather
ο πατέρας (pat**e**ras)	father
ο κυβερνήτης (keevern**ee**tees)	captain
	(of aeroplane)

Feminine endings of nouns

The most common endings of feminine nouns are
−**α** (a), −**η** (ee), e.g.

η μητέρα (meet**e**ra)　　　　mother
η Κρήτη (kr**ee**tee)　　　　　Crete

Neuter endings of nouns

The most common neuter endings are: −**ο** (o), −**ι** (ee),
e.g.

το κτίριο (kt**ee**reeo)　　　　building
το πορτοκάλι (portok**a**lee)　　orange (fruit)

Plurals

• •

The article 'the' changes in the plural. For masculine
(**ο**) and feminine (**η**) nouns it becomes **οι** (ee).
For neuter nouns (**το**) it becomes **τα** (ta).

Nouns have different endings in the plural.
Masculine nouns change their endings to −**οι** (ee),
e.g.

ο βράχος (vr**a**khos)　　　**οι βράχοι** (vr**a**khee)

Feminine nouns change their endings to −**ες** (es), e.g.
η κυρία (ker**ee**a)　　　**οι κυρίες** (ker**ee**-es)

165

Neuter nouns change their endings to −α (a), e.g.

   το κτίριο (kt**ee**reeo)   τα κτίρια (kt**ee**reea)

There are many exceptions to the above rules, such as:

   ο άντρας (**a**ndhras)   οι άντρες (**a**ndhres)

Adjectives

••

An adjective is a word that describes or gives extra information about a person or thing, e.g. 'small', 'pretty' or 'practical'. Greek adjectives have endings that change according to the gender and number of the noun they describe, e.g.

ο καλός πατέρας	the good father
(kal**o**s pat**e**ras)	
η καλή κυρία (kal**ee** ker**ee**a)	the good lady
οι καλοί πατέρες	the good fathers
(kal**ee** pat**e**res)	
οι καλές κυρίες	the good ladies
(kal**e**s ker**ee**-es)	

In the Greek-English dictionary section of this book, all adjectives are given with their endings clearly shown, e.g.

   κρύος/α/ο (kr**ee**-os/a/o)   cold

By far the most common adjective endings are **–ος** (os) for masculine, **–α** (a) for feminine and **–ο** (o) for neuter nouns.

Possessive adjectives

In Greek, adjectives go before the noun they describe, but the possessive adjectives (my, your, his, etc.) follow the noun. They don't change according to the gender and number of the noun. The article is still added in front of the noun.

my	**μου**	moo
your	**σου**	soo
his	**του**	too
her	**της**	tees
its	**του**	too
our	**μας**	mas
your (plural) (This is also the polite form)	**σας**	sas
their	**τους**	toos

my key	**το κλειδί μου** (to kleeth**ee** moo)
your room	**το δωμάτιό σας** (to dhom**a**tee**o** sas)

Verbs

•••

A verb is a word used to say what someone or
something does or what happens, e.g. 'sing', 'walk',
'rain'. Unlike verbs in English, Greek verbs have
a different ending for each person, singular and
plural. The most essential verbs in Greek are the
verbs **είμαι** 'I am' and **έχω** 'I have'.

Grammar

to be

είμαι	I am	**ee**me
είσαι	you are	**ee**se
είναι	he/she/it is	**ee**ne
είμαστε	we are	**ee**maste
είστε	you are	**ee**ste*
είναι	they are	**ee**ne

* This form is also used when addressing someone
you do not know very well; it is generally referred to
as the polite plural (like the French 'vous').

Note: While in English it is necessary to use the
personal pronoun, i.e. we, you etc, in order to
distinguish between 'we are', 'you are' etc, in Greek
this function is carried out by the different endings of
the verb itself. Thus, in Greek, 'we are' and 'they are'
can be simply **είμαστε** (**ee**maste), **είναι** (**ee**ne).

to have

έχω	I have	**e**kho
έχεις	you have	**e**khees
έχει	he/she/it has	**e**khee
έχουμε	we have	**e**khoome
έχετε	you have	**e**khete
έχουν	they have	**e**khoon

Note: As above, 'I have' can be expressed in Greek with simply the verb έχω; each ending is particular to a specific person.

Verbs in Greek, in the active voice, end in –ω (o) or –ώ (o). This is the ending with which they generally appear in dictionaries. Note that in everyday speech a more usual ending for –ώ (o) is –άω (ao). If a verb does not have an active voice form, in a dictionary it will appear with the ending –μαι (-me), e.g.

λυπάμαι (leep**a**me) to be sad or sorry
θυμάμαι (theem**a**me) to remember.

The verb αγαπώ (aghap**o**) 'to love' has typical endings for verbs ending in –ώ (-o), while those ending in –ω (-o) follow the pattern of έχω (**e**kho) above.

αγαπώ/άω (aghap**o**/**a**o)	I love
αγαπάς (aghap**a**s)	you love
αγαπά (aghap**a**)	he/she/it loves

169

αγαπούμε (aghapoome)	we love
αγαπάτε (aghapate)	you love
αγαπούν (aghapoon)	they love

Negative

• •

To make a sentence negative, you put δεν (dhen) immediately before the verb, e.g.

| I don't know | δεν ξέρω | dhen ksero |
| I have no... | δεν έχω... | dhen ekho |

Future

• •

The future tense is made by adding θα (tha) immediately before the verb, e.g.

| θα πάω tha pao | I shall go |
| δε θα πάω dhe tha pao | I shall not go |

Forms of address

∙∙

In Greek, there are two ways of addressing people, depending on their age, social or professional status, and how formal or informal the relationship is between two people. For example, an older person will probably speak to a much younger one using the singular (informal) but the younger person will use the plural (formal) unless well acquainted. Two friends will speak to each other using the informal singular:

Τι κάνεις; (tee ka**nees**?)	How are you?
Καλά, εσύ; (kal**a** es**ee**?)	Fine, and you?

But two acquaintances will address each other in a more formal way, using the plural:

Τι κάνετε; (tee k**a**nete?)	How are you?
Καλά, εσείς; (kal**a**, es**ee**s?)	Fine, and you?

Personal pronouns

••

A pronoun is a word used to refer to someone or something that has been mentioned earlier, e.g. 'it', 'they', 'him'. There are times when a personal pronoun needs to be used in Greek, e.g. in order to establish the sex of the person or the gender of the thing referred to, i.e. he, she or it.

εγώ	I	egho
εσύ	you	esee
αυτός	he	aftos
αυτή	she	aftee
αυτό	it	afto
εμείς	we	emees
εσείς	you	esees
αυτοί	they (masculine)	aftee
αυτές	they (feminine)	aftes
αυτά	they (neuter)	afta

Thus:

αυτός έχει (aftos ekhee)   he has
αυτή έχει (aftee ekhee)   she has

Public holidays

January 1	**Πρωτοχρονιά** New Year's Day
January 6	**Θεοφάνεια** Epiphany
Late February/ early March (40 days before Easter)	**Καθαρά Δευτέρα (Αρχή Σαρακοστής)** Ash Monday
March 25	**Ο Ευαγγελισμός/Εθνική γιορτή της Ανεξαρτησίας** Annunciation and Greek Independence Day
April/May (Good Friday to Easter Monday)	**Πάσχα** Easter
May 1	**Εργατική Ημέρα Πρωτομαγιάς** Labour Day
May/June	**Πεντηκοστή** Whit Monday
August 15	**Ανάληψη (της Παναγίας)** Assumption (of the Virgin Mary)
October 28	The "Ochi" Day: 2nd World War Memorial Day
December 25	**Χριστούγεννα** Christmas Day
December 26	**Δεύτερη Ημέρα των Χριστουγέννων** Boxing Day/St Stephen's Day

English – Greek

A		
a (masculine ο words)	ένας	enas
(feminine η words)	μία	meea
(neuter το words)	ένα	ena
about: *a book about Athens*	ένα βιβλίο για την Αθήνα	ena veevleeo ya teen Atheena
at about ten o'clock	περίπου στις δέκα	pereepoo stees dheka
above	πάνω από	pano apo
accident	το ατύχημα	to ateekheema
accommodation	το κατάλυμα	to kataleema
address	η διεύθυνση	ee dheeeftheensee
admission charge	η είσοδος	ee eesodhos
adult	ο ενήλικος	o eneeleekos
advance: *in advance*	προκατα–βολικώς	prokatavoleekos
Aegean Sea	το Αιγαίο (πέλαγος)	to egheo (pelaghos)
after	μετά	meta
afternoon	το απόγευμα	to apoyevma
again	πάλι/ξανά	palee/ksana
ago: *a week ago*	πριν μια βδομάδα	preen mya vdhomadha
air conditioning	ο κλιματισμός	o kleemateesmos
airline	η αεροπορική εταιρία	ee aeroporeekee etereea
airplane	το αεροπλάνο	to aeroplano
airport	το αεροδρόμιο	to aerodhromeeo
airport bus	το λεωφορείο για/ το αεροδρό–μειο	to leoforeeo ya/ to aerodhromeeo
air ticket	το αεροπορικό εισιτήριο	to aeroporeeko eeseeteereeo
alarm (emergency)	ο συναγερμός	o seenayermos
alarm clock	το ξυπνητήρι	to kseepneeteeree
alcohol	το αλκοόλ	to alko-ol

alcohol-free	χωρίς αλκοόλ	khorees alko-ol
alcoholic	οινοπνευμα- τώδης	eenopnevma- todhees
all	όλος	olos
all the milk	όλο το γάλα	olo to ghala
all the time	όλον τον καιρό	olon ton kero
allergic to	αλλεργικός σε	aleryekos se
all right (agreed)	εντάξει	endaksee
also	επίσης	epeesees
always	πάντα	panda
ambulance	το ασθενοφόρο	to asthenoforo
America	η Αμερική	ee amereekee
American	ο Αμερικανός/ η Αμερικανίδα	o amereekanos/ ee amereeka-needha
and	και	ke
angry	θυμωμένος	theemomenos
another	άλλος	alos
another beer	άλλη μία μπίρα	alee meea beera
answer	η απάντηση	ee apandeesee

to answer	απαντώ	apando
answerphone	ο αυτόματος τηλεφωνητής	o aftomatos teelefoneetees
antibiotics	τα αντιβιοτικά	ta andeeveeo-teeka
antiseptic	το αντισηπτικό	to andeeseep-teeko
apartment	το διαμέρισμα	to dheeamer-eesma
arm	το μπράτσο	to bratso
around	γύρω	yeero
arrivals	οι αφίξεις	ee afeeksees
to arrive	φτάνω	ftano
aspirin	η ασπιρίνη	ee aspeereenee
asthma	το άσθμα	to asthma
at	σε	se
at the (masculine, neuter)	στο	sto
at the (feminine)	στη	stee

English – Greek

attractive (person)	ελκυστικός	ellkeesteekos	
Australia	η Αυστραλία	ee afstraleea	
Australian	ο Αυστραλός/ η Αυστραλέζα	o afstralos/ ee afstraleza	
automatic	αυτόματος	aftomatos	
autumn	το φθινόπωρο	to ftheenoporo	
awful	φοβερός	foveros	

B

baby	το μωρό	to moro	
baby's bottle	το μπιμπερό	to beebero	
baby seat (in car)	το παιδικό κάθισμα	to pedheeko katheesma	
baby-sitter	η μπεϊμπισίτερ	ee babysitter	
baby wipes	τα υγρά μαντηλάκια για μωρά	ta eeghra mandeelakya ya mora	
back (of a person)	η πλάτη	ee platee	

bad (off food) (of weather)	χαλασμένος κακός	khalasmenos kakos	
bag (small) (suitcase)	η τσάντα η βαλίτσα	ee tsanda ee valeetsa	
baggage	οι αποσκευές	ee aposkeves	
bank	το τράπεζα	to trapeza	
banknote	το χαρτονόμισμα	to khartonomeesma	
bar	το μπαρ	to bar	
bath (tub)	το μπάνιο	to banyo	
to take a bath	κάνω μπάνιο	kano banyo	
bathroom	το μπάνιο	to banyo	
battery	η μπαταρία	ee batareea	
beach	η πλαζ/ η παραλία	ee plaz/ ee paraleea	
beautiful	όμορφος	omorfos	
because	επειδή	epeedhee	
bed	το κρεβάτι	to krevatee	
double bed	διπλό κρεβάτι	dheeplo krevatee	
single bed	μονό κρεβάτι	mono krevatee	

twin beds	δύο μονά κρεβάτια	dheeo mona krevatya
bedroom	η κρεβατοκά- μαρα	ee krevatokamara
beer	η μπύρα	ee beera
before (time)	πριν (από)	preen (apo)
(place)	μπροστά από	brosta apo
to begin	αρχίζω	arkheezo
behind	πίσω από	peeso apo
to believe	πιστεύω	peestevo
below	κάτω από	kato apo
beside	δίπλα	dheepla
best	ο καλύτερος	o kaleeteros
better (than)	καλύτερος (από)	kaleeteros (apo)
between	μεταξύ	metaksee
bicycle	το ποδήλατο	to podheelato
big	μεγάλος	meghalos
bigger	μεγαλύτερος	meghaleeteros
bill	ο λογαριασμός	o loghariasmos

birthday	τα γενέθλια	ta yenethleea
happy birthday!	χρόνια πολλά	khronya pola
biscuit	το μπισκότο	to beeskoto
bit: a bit (of)	λίγο	leegho
bite (insect)	το τσίμπημα	to tseebeema
bitten: I have been bitten	με δάγκωσε	me dhangkose

bitter	πικρός	peekros
black	μαύρος	mavros
blocked (pipe)	βουλωμένος	voolomenos
(nose)	κλειστή	kleestee
blood pressure	η πίεση αίματος	ee peeyesee ematos
blouse	η μπλούζα	ee blooza
blow-dry	στέγνωμα	steghnoma
blue	γαλάζιος/ μπλε	ghalazyos/ble
boat (small)	η βάρκα	ee varka
(ship)	το πλοίο	to pleeo
to boil	βράζω	vrazo

English – Greek

book	η το βιβλίο	to veevleeo
to book	κλείνω	kleeno
booking: to make a booking	κλείνω θέση	kleeno thesee
booking office (railways, airlines, etc.)	το εκδοτήριο	to ekdhoteereeo
(theatre)	το ταμείο	to tameeo
bookshop	το βιβλιοπωλείο	to veevleeopoleeo
boots	οι μπότες	ee botes
boring	βαρετός	varetos
bottle	το μπουκάλι	to bookalee
box office	το ταμείο	to tameeo
boy	το αγόρι	to aghoree
boyfriend	ο φίλος	o feelos
to brake	φρενάρω	frenaro
brakes	τα φρένα	ta frena

bread (wholemeal)	το ψωμί	to psomee
	ψωμί ολικής αλέσεως	psomee oleekees aleseos
to break	σπάζω	spazo
breakfast	το πρωινό	to proeeno
breast	το στήθος	to steethos
to breathe	αναπνέω	anapneo
bride	η νύφη	ee neefee
bridegroom	ο γαμπρός	o ghambros
to bring	φέρνω	ferno
Britain	η Βρετανία	ee vretaneea
British	ο Βρετανός/ η Βρετανίδα	o vretanos/ ee vretaneedha
broken	σπασμένος	spasmenos
broken down	χαλασμένος	khalasmenos
brother	ο αδελφός	o adhelfos
brown	καφέ	kafe
bulb (light)	ο γλόμπος	o ghlobos
bureau de change (bank)	ξένο συνάλλαγμα	kseno seenalaghma

English – Greek

bus	το λεωφορείο	to leoforeeo
business	η δουλειά	ee dhoolya
business centre	το εμπορικό κέντρο	to emboreeko kendro
bus station	ο σταθμός του λεωφορείου	o stathmos too leoforeeoo
bus stop	η στάση του λεωφορείου	ee stasee too leoforeeoo
bus terminal	το τέρμα του λεωφορείου	to terma too leoforeeoo
busy	απασχολη-μένος	apaskholemenos
but	αλλά	ala
to buy	αγοράζω	aghorazo
C		
cab	το ταξί	to taksee
café	το καφενείο	to kafeneeo
cake	το γλύκισμα	o ghleekeesma
to call	φωνάζω	fonazo

call (telephone)	η κλήση	ee kleesee
long-distance call	η υπεραστική κλήση	ee eeperasteekee kleesee
calm	ήσυχος	eesekhos
camera	η φωτογραφική μηχανή	ee fotoghrafeekee meekhanee
to camp	κατασκηνώνω	kataskeenono
campsite	το κάμπινγκ	to camping
can: I can	μπορώ	boro
you can	μπορείς	borees
he can	μπορεί	boree
we can	μπορούμε	boroome
can (of food)	η κονσέρβα	ee konserva
Canada	ο Καναδάς	o kanadhas
Canadian	ο Καναδός/η Καναδή	o Kanadhos/ee Kanadhee
to cancel	ακυρώνω	akeerono
car	το αυτοκίνητο	to aftokeeneeto
car ferry	το φέρημπότ	to fereebot

English	Greek		
car keys	τα κλειδιά αυτοκινήτου	ta kleedhya aftokeeneetoo	
car park	το πάρκινγκ	to parking	
card	η κάρτα	ee karta	
careful	προσεκτικός	prosekteekos	
carriage (railway)	το βαγόνι	to vaghonee	
to carry	κουβαλώ	koovalo	
to cash (cheque)	εξαργυρώνω	eksaryeerono	
cash	τα μετρητά	ta metreeta	
cash desk	το ταμείο	to tameeo	
cash dispenser	το ΑΤΜ	to ey tee em	
castle	το κάστρο	to kastro	
casualty department	τμήμα για επείγοντα περιστατικά	tmeema ya epeeghonda pereestateeka	
cat	η γάτα	ee ghata	
catalogue	ο κατάλογος	o kataloghos	
to catch (bus, train, etc.)	πιάνω	pyano	
Catholic	καθολικός	katholeekos	

English	Greek		
cents (euro)	λεπτά	lepta	
centimetre	το εκατοστό	to ekastosto	
central	κεντρικός	kendreekos	
centre	το κέντρο	to kendro	
century	ο αιώνας	o eonas	
certificate	το πιστοποιητικό	to peestopee- ee teeko	
chain	η αλυσίδα	ee aleeseedha	
chair	η καρέκλα	ee karekla	
champagne	η σαμπάνια	ee sambanya	
change (money)	η αλλαγή	ee alaghee	
	τα ρέστα	ta resta	
to change	αλλάζω	alazo	
charge (price)	η τιμή	ee teemee	
charge (electric)	η φόρτωση	ee forteesee	
I've run out of charge	έμεινα από μπαταρία	emeena apo batareea	
cheap	φτηνός	fteenos	
to check	ελέγχω	elenkho	

English	Greek	Pronunciation
to check in	περνώ από τον έλεγχο	perno apo ton elenkho
	εισιτηρίων	eseeteereeon
cheers!	γεια μας!	ya mas!
cheese	το τυρί	to teeree
chemist's	το φαρμακείο	to farmakeeo
cheque	η επιταγή	ee epeetaghee
cheque card	η κάρτα επιταγών	ee karta epeetaghon
child	το παιδί	to pedhee
children	τα παιδιά	ta pedhya
chips	πατάτες τηγανητές	patates teeghaneetes
chocolate	η σοκολάτα	ee sokolata
Christmas	τα Χριστούγεννα	ta khreestooyena
merry Christmas!	καλά Χριστούγεννα!	kala khreestooyena
church	η εκκλησία	ee ekleeseea
cigarette	το τσιγάρο	to tseegharo
cinema	ο κινηματογράφος	o keeneematoghrafos
city	η πόλη	ee polee
clean	καθαρός	katharos
to clean	καθαρίζω	kathareezo
client	ο πελάτης/ η πελάτισσα	o pelatees/ ee pelateesa
climbing	η ορειβασία	ee oreevaseea
clock	το ρολόι	to roloee
to close	κλείνω	kleeno
close adj (near)	κοντινός	kondeenos
closed (weather)	αποπνυχτικός	apopneekhteekos
clothes	κλειστός	kleestos
cloudy	τα ρούχα	ta rookha
	συννεφιασμένος	seenefyasmenos
coach (railway)	το βαγόνι	to vaghonee
(bus)	το πούλμαν	to poolman
coach station	ο σταθμός λεωφορείων	o stathmos leoforeeon

English - Greek

English	Greek	Pronunciation
coast	η ακτή	ee aktee
coat	το παλτό	to palto
coffee	ο καφές	o kafes
black coffee	σκέτος καφές	sketos kafes
white coffee	καφές με γάλα	kafes me ghala
cold	κρύος	kreeos
I have a cold	είμαι κρυωμένος	eeme kreeomenos
colour	το χρώμα	to khroma
to come	έρχομαι	erkhome
to come back	γυρίζω	yereezo
to come in	μπαίνω	beno
comfortable	αναπαυτικός	anapafteekos
company (firm)	η εταιρία	ee eterea
compartment (train)	το βαγόνι	to vaghonee
to complain	παραπονούμαι	paraponoome
computer	το κομπιούτερ	to kompyooter
concert	η συναυλία	ee seenavleea
condom	το προφυλακτικό	to profeelakteeko
to confirm	επιβεβαιώνω	epeveono
congratulations!	συγχαρητήρια	seenkhareeteerea
connection (trains, etc)	η σύνδεση	ee seendhesee
consulate	το προξενείο	to prokseneeo
to contact	έρχομαι σε επαφή	erkhome se epafee
contact lenses	οι φακοί επαφής	ee fakee epafees
contraceptives	τα αντισυλ-ληπτικά	ta andeesee-leepteeka
contract	το συμβόλαιο	to seemvoleo
to cook	μαγειρεύω	magheerevo
cooker	η κουζίνα	ee koozeena
cool	δροσερός	dhroseros
to copy (photocopy)	φωτοτυπώ	fototeepo
copy noun	το αντίγραφο	to andeeghrafo

English	Greek	Pronunciation
corner	η γωνία	ee ghonea
cosmetics	τα καλλυντικά	ta kaleendeeka
to cost	κοστίζω	kosteezo
how much does it cost?	πόσο κάνει;	poso kanee?
cough	ο βήχας	o veekhas
country	η χώρα	ee khora
(not town)	η εξοχή	ee eksokhee
couple (two people)	το ζευγάρι	to zevgharee
course (meal)	το πιάτο	to pyato
cousin	ο εξάδελφος/ η εξαδέλφη	o eksadhelfos/ ee eksadhelfee
cover charge	το κουβέρ	to koover
to crash	συγκρούομαι	seengkrooome
crash	η σύγκρουση	ee seengroosee
crash helmet	το κράνος	to kranos
credit (on mobile phone)	οι μονάδες	ee monadhes

English	Greek	Pronunciation
credit card	η πιστωτική κάρτα	ee peestoteekee karta
to cross	διασχίζω	dheeaskheezo
crowded	γεμάτος	yematos
cruise	το κρουαζιέρα	ee krooazyera
cup	το φλυτζάνι	to fleedzanee
current (electric)	το ρεύμα	to revma
customer	ο πελάτης	o pelatees
to cut	κόβω	kovo
to cycle	ποδηλατώ	podheelato
cystitis	η κυστίτιδα	ee keesteeteedha

D

English	Greek	Pronunciation
daily	ημερήσιος	eemereeseeos
dairy products	τα γαλακτοκο- μικά προϊόντα	ta ghalaktoko- meeka proeeonda
damage	η ζημιά	ee zeemya
damp	υγρός	eeghros
dance	ο χορός	o khoros

English	Greek	Pronunciation
to dance	χορεύω	khorevo
danger	ο κίνδυνος	o keendheenos
dangerous	επικίνδυνος	epeekeendheenos
dark (colour)	σκούρο	skooro
date	η ημερομηνία	ee eemeromee-neea
date of birth	η ημερομηνία γεννήσεως	ee eemeromee-neea yeneseos
daughter	η κόρη	ee koree
day	η μέρα	ee mera
dead	νεκρός	nekros
dear	αγαπητός	aghapeetos
(expensive)	ακριβός	akreevos
debit card	η κάρτα ανάληψης	ee karta analeepsees
decaffeinated	χωρίς καφεΐνη	khores kafe-eenee
deck chair	η ξαπλώστρα	ee ksaplostra
deep	βαθύς	vathees
delay	η καθυστέρηση	ee katheesteresee
delayed	καθυστερη-μένος	katheesteree-menos
delicious	νόστιμος	nosteemos
dentist	ο/η οδοντία-τρος	o/ee odhondee-atros
deodorant	το αποσμητικό	to aposmeeteeko
department store	το πολυκατά-στημα	to poleekata-steema
departure	η αναχώρηση	ee anakhoreesee
diabetic	διαβητικός	dheeaveeteekos
to dial	παίρνω αριθμό	perno areethmo
dialling code	ο τηλεφωνικός κωδικός	o teelefoneekos kodheekas
diet	η δίαιτα	ee dhee-eta
I'm on a diet	κάνω δίαιτα	kano dhee-eta
different	διαφορετικός	dheeaforeteekos
difficult	δύσκολος	dheeskolos
digital camera	η ψηφιακή φωτογραφική μηχανή	ee psefeeakee fotoghrafeekee meekhanee

English	Greek	
dining room	η τραπεζαρία	ee trapezarea
dinner	το δείπνο	to dheepno
direct	άμεσος	amesos
directory (telephone)	ο τηλεφωνικός κατάλογος	o teelefoneekos kataloghos
dirty	βρώμικος	vromeekos
disabled	ανάπηρος	anapeeros
discount	η έκπτωση	ee ekptosee
divorced	χωρισμένος/ χωρισμένη	khoreesmenos/ khoreesmenee
dizzy	ζαλισμένος	zaleesmenos
to do: I do	κάνω	kano
	κάνεις	kanees
doctor	ο/η γιατρός	o/ee yatros
documents	τα έγγραφα	ta engrafa
dog	το σκυλί	to skeelee
dollar	το δολάριο	to dholareeo
door	η πόρτα	ee porta
double	διπλός	dheeplos

English	Greek	
double bed	το διπλό κρεββάτι	to dheeplo krevatee
double room	το δίκλινο δωμάτιο	to dheekleeno dhomateeo
down: to go down	κατεβαίνω	kateveno
downstairs	κάτω	kato
dress	το φόρεμα	to forema
to dress	ντύνομαι	deenome
drink noun	το ποτό	to poto
to have a drink	παίρνω ένα ποτό	perno ena poto
to drink	πίνω	peeno
drinking water	το πόσιμο νερό	to poseemo nero
to drive	οδηγώ	odheegho
driver	ο οδηγός	o odheeghos
driving licence	η άδεια οδήγησης	ee adheea odheegheesees
to drown	πνίγομαι	pneeghome

English – Greek

English	Greek	
drug (illegal)	το ναρκωτικό	to narkoteeko
(medicine)	το φάρμακο	to farmako
drunk	μεθυσμένος	metheesmenos
dry adj	στεγνός	steghnos
to dry	στεγνώνω	steghnono
dry-cleaners	το καθαρι-	to kathareestee-
	στήριο	reeo
during	κατά τη	kata tee
	διάρκεια	dheearkeea
E		
each	κάθε	kathe
ear	το αυτί	to aftee
earache: I have	με πονάει το	me ponaee to
an earache	αυτί μου	aftee moo
earlier	νωρίτερα	noreetera
early	νωρίς	norees
east	η ανατολή	ee anatolee
Easter	το Πάσχα	to paskha
easy	εύκολος	efkolos

English	Greek	
to eat	τρώω	troo
electronic	ηλεκτρονικός;/	eelektroneekos/
	ή/ό	ee/o
e-mail	το e-mail	to e-mail
e-mail address	η e-mail	ee e-mail
embassy	διεύθυνση	dheeeftheensee
	η πρεσβεία	ee presveea
emergency: it's	είναι επείγον	eene epeeghon
an emergency	περιστατικό	pereestateeko
empty	άδειος	adheeos
end	το τέλος	to telos
engaged	αρραβωνιασ-	aravonyas-
(to marry)	μένος/η	menos/ee
engine	η μηχανή	ee meekhanee
England	η Αγγλία	ee angleea
English (thing)	αγγλικός	angleekos
Englishman/	ο Άγγλος/	o anglos/
woman	η Αγγλίδα	ee angleedha
to enjoy oneself	διασκεδάζω	dhyaskedhazo
enough	αρκετά	arketa

English	Greek	Pronunciation
enough bread	αρκετό ψωμί	arketo psomee
enquiry desk/office	το γραφείο πληροφοριών	to ghrafeeo pleerofforeeon
to enter	μπαίνω	beno
entrance	η είσοδος	ee eesodhos
entrance fee	η τιμή εισόδου	ee teemee eesodhoo
essential	απαραίτητος	apareteetos
euro	ευρώ	evro
Europe	η Ευρώπη	ee evropee
evening	το βράδυ	to vradhee
this evening	απόψε	apopse
in the evening	το βράδυ	to vradhee
every	κάθε	kathe
everyone	όλοι	olee
everything	όλα	ola
excellent	εξαιρετικός	eksereteekos
except	εκτός από	ektos apo
exchange rate	η τιμή του συναλλάγματος	ee teemee too seenalaghmatos
excuse me	με συγχωρείτε	me seeghkhoreete
exit	η έξοδος	ee eksodhos
expensive	ακριβός	akreevos
extra: it costs	κοστίζει	kosteezee
extra	επιπλέον	epeepleon
extra money	περισσότερα χρήματα	pereesotera khreemata
eyes	τα μάτια	ta matya

F

English	Greek	Pronunciation
face	το πρόσωπο	to prosopo
facilities	οι ευκολίες	ee efkoleeyes
to faint	λιποθυμώ	leepotheemo
to fall	πέφτω	pefto
he/she has fallen	έπεσε	epese
family	η οικογένεια	ee eekoyeneea
fan (electric)	ο ανεμιστήρας	o anemeesteeras
far	μακριά	makreea
fare (bus, train)	το εισιτήριο	to eeseeteereeo

English – Greek

English – Greek

English	Greek	Pronunciation
fast	γρήγορα	gheeghora
father	ο πατέρας	o pateras
fault (mistake)	το λάθος	to lathos
it is not my fault	δε φταίω εγώ	dhe fteo egho
fax	το φαξ	fax
to feel	αισθάνομαι	esthanome
I feel sick	θέλω να κάνω εμετό	thelo na kano emeto
female	θηλυκός	theeleekos
ferry	το φεριμπότ	to fereebot
to fetch	φέρνω	ferno
fever	ο πυρετός	o peeretos
fiancé(e)	ο αρραβωνιαστικός/ η αρραβωνιαστικιά	o aravonya-steekos/ ee aravon-yasteekya
to fill	γεμίζω	yemeezo
fill it up! (car)	γεμίστε το	yemeeste to
fillet	το φιλέτο	to feeleto

English	Greek	Pronunciation
film (for camera)	το φιλμ	to feelm
(in cinema)	η ταινία	ee teneea
to finish	τελειώνω	teleeono
fire (heater)	η θερμάστρα	ee thermastra
fire!	φωτιά!	fotya!
fire brigade	η πυροσβεστική	ee peerosvesteekee
fire extinguisher	ο πυροσβεστήρας	o peerosvesteeras
first	πρώτος	protos
first aid	οι πρώτες βοήθειες	ee protes voeetheeyes
first class (seat, etc)	η πρώτη θέση	ee protee thesee
first name	το όνομα	to onoma
fish	το ψάρι	to psaree
to fish	ψαρεύω	psarevo
fit (healthy)	υγιής	eeyees
to fix (arrange)	φτιάχνω	ftyakhno
fizzy (drink)	κανονίζω	kanoneezo
	αεριούχο	aeryookho

English	Greek	
flat (apartment)	το διαμέρισμα	to dheeame-reesma
flight	η πτήση	ee pteesee
floor	το πάτωμα	to patoma
(storey)	ο όροφος	o orofos
flower	το λουλούδι	to looloodhee
flu	η γρίπη	ee ghreepee
to fly	πετώ	peto
food	το φαγητό	to fa-yeeto
food poisoning	η τροφική δηλητηρίαση	ee trofeekee dhee-leeteereeasee
foot	το πόδι	to podhee
football	το ποδόσφαιρο	to podhosfero
for	για	ya
foreign	ξένος	ksenos
to forget	ξεχνώ	ksekhno
fork	το πιρούνι	to peeroonee
(in road)	η διακλάδωση	ee dheeakladhosee
fracture (of bone)	το κάταγμα	to kataghma
France	η Γαλλία	ee ghaleea

English	Greek	
free (costing nothing)	ελεύθερος	eleftheros
	δωρεάν	dhorean
French (thing)	γαλλικός	ghaleekos
frequent	συχνός	seekhnos
fresh	φρέσκος	freskos
fried	τηγανητός	teeghaneetos
friend	ο φίλος/η φίλη	o feelos/ee feelee
from	από	apo
front (part)	το μπροστινό (μέρος)	to brosteeno (meros)
in front	μπροστά	brosta
fruit	τα φρούτα	ta froota
fruit juice	ο χυμός φρούτων	o kheemos frooton
full	γεμάτος	yematos
full board	(η) πλήρης διατροφή	(ee) pleerees dheeatrofee
funny	αστείος	asteeos

English – Greek

G

gallery (art)	η πινακοθήκη	ee peenakothee-kee
game (to eat)	το παιγνίδι το κυνήγι	to peghneedhee to keeneeghee
garage (for parking car)	το γκαράζ	to garaz
garden	ο κήπος	o keepos
gate (at airport)	η έξοδος	ee eksodhos
gents (toilet)	ανδρών	andhron
genuine	γνήσιος	ghneeseeos
to get (fetch)	παίρνω	perno
	φέρνω	ferno
to get in (car, etc.)	μπαίνω	beno
to get off	κατεβαίνω από	kateveno apo
to get on (from bus)	ανεβαίνω στο λεωφορείο	aneveno sto leoforeeo
(bus)		
gift	το δώρο	to dhoro
girl	το κορίτσι	to koreetsee

girlfriend	η φίλη/ η φιλενάδα	ee feelee/ ee feelenadha
to give	δίνω	dheeno
glass (to drink from)	το ποτήρι	to poteeree
a glass of water	ένα ποτήρι νερό	ena poteeree nero
glasses (spectacles)	τα γυαλιά	ta yalya
to go	πηγαίνω	peegheno
I go/I am going	πηγαίνω	peegheno
you go/you are going	πηγαίνεις	peeghenees
we go/we are going	πηγαίνουμε	peeghenoome
to go back	γυρίζω πίσω	yeereezo peeso
to go in	μπαίνω	beno
to go out	βγαίνω	vgheno
gold	ο χρυσός	o khreesos
(made of gold)	χρυσός	khreesos

good	καλός	kalos
good afternoon	χαίρετε	kherete
goodbye	αντίο	adeeo
good day	καλημέρα	kaleemera
good evening	καλησπέρα	kaleespera
good morning	καλημέρα	kaleemera
good night	καληνύχτα	kaleeneekhta
grandfather	ο παππούς	o papoos
grandmother	η γιαγιά	ee yaya
grapes	τα σταφύλια	ta stafeelya
great	μεγάλος	meghalos
Greece	η Ελλάδα	ee eladha
Greek (person)	ο Έλληνας/ η Ελληνίδα	o eleenas/ ee eleeneedha
Greek adj	ελληνικός	eleeneekos
green	πράσινος	praseenos
grey	γκρίζος	greezos
grocer's	το μπακάλικο το παντοπω-λείο	to bakaleeko to pandopoleeo
group	η ομάδα	ee omadha
guest	ο φιλοξενού-μενος	o feeloksenoo-menos
guide	ο/η ξεναγός	o/ee ksenaghos
guidebook	ο οδηγός	o odheeghos

H

hair	τα μαλλιά	ta malya
hairdresser	ο κομμωτής/ η κομμώτρια	o komotees/ ee komotreea
half	το μισό	to meeso
half an hour	μισή ώρα	meesee ora
half board	(η) ημιδιατροφή	(ee) eemeedhee-atrofee
half price	μισή τιμή	meesee teemee
hand	το χέρι	to kheree
handbag	η τσάντα	ee tsanda
handicapped	ανάπηρος	anapeeros

English – Greek

English – Greek

English	Greek	
handkerchief (tissue)	το μαντήλι	to mandeelee
	το χαρτομά-ντηλο	to khartoman-deelo
hand luggage	η χειραποσκευή	ee kheeraposkevee
hand-made	χειροποίητος	kheeropee-eetos
to happen	συμβαίνω	seemveno
what happened?	τι συνέβη;	tee seenevee?
happy	χαρούμενος	kharoomenos
hard (difficult)	δύσκολος	dheeskolos
hat	το καπέλο	to kapelo
he	αυτός	aftos
head	το κεφάλι	to kefalee
headache: I have a headache	έχω πονοκέφαλο	ekho ponokefalo
health	η υγεία	ee eegheea
to hear	ακούω	akoo-o
heart	η καρδιά	ee kardhya
heating	η θέρμανση	ee thermansee
heavy	βαρύς	varees

English	Greek	
hello	γεια σας	ya sas
to help	βοηθώ	voeetho
help!	βοήθεια	voeetheea
here	εδώ	edho
to hire	νοικιάζω	neekyazo
to hold	κρατώ	krato
hold-up	η καθυστέρηση	ee katheesteresee
holidays	οι διακοπές	ee dheeakopes
home	το σπίτι	sto speetee
at home	στο σπίτι	sto speetee
to hope	ελπίζω	elpeezo
hospital	το νοσοκομείο	to nosokomeeo
hot	ζεστός	zestos
I'm hot	ζεσταίνομαι	zestenome
it's hot	έχει ζέστη	ekhee zestee
hot water	το ζεστό νερό	to zesto nero
hotel	το ξενοδοχείο	to ksenodhokheeo
hour	η ώρα	ee ora
house	το σπίτι	to speetee
house wine	το κρασί χύμα	to krasee kheema

how	πώς	pos
how long?	πόση ώρα;	posee ora?
how much?	πόσο;	poso?
how many?	πόσα;	posa?
how are you?	πώς είστε;	pos eeste?
I'm hungry:	πεινώ	peeno
to hurry: I'm in a hurry:	βιάζομαι	vyazome
to hurt: that hurts	με πονάει	me ponaee
husband	ο σύζυγος	o seezeeghos
I	εγώ	egho
ice	ο πάγος	o paghos
ice cream/ice lolly	το παγωτό	to paghoto
if	αν	an
ill	άρρωστος	arostos

immediately	αμέσως	amesos
impossible	αδύνατο	adheenato
in (inside)	μέσα	mesa
(into)	σε	se
(with countries, towns)	στο/	sto/
	στη/	stee/
	στο	sto
infectious	μεταδοτικός	metadhoteekos
information	οι πληροφορίες	ee pleeroforeeyes
injured	τραυματισμένος	travmateesmenos
insect	το έντομο	to endomo
inside (interior)	το εσωτερικό	to esotereeko
inside the car	μέσα στο αυτοκίνητο	mesa sto aftokeeneeto
it's inside	είναι μέσα	eene mesa
insurance	η ασφάλεια	ee asfalea
insured	ασφαλισμένος	asfaleesmenos
interesting	ενδιαφέρων	endheeaferon
international	διεθνής	dhee-ethnees

English – Greek

to invite	προσκαλώ	proskalo	
Ireland	η Ιρλανδία	ee eerlandheea	
Irish (person)	ο Ιρλανδός/	o eerlandhos/	
	η Ιρλανδή	ee eerlandhee	
iron (for clothes)	το σίδερο	to seedhero	
island	το νησί	to neesee	
it	το	to	
Italy	η Ιταλία	ee eetaleea	
itch	η φαγούρα	ee faghoora	

J			
jacket	το μπουφάν	to boofan	
jam	η μαρμελάδα	ee marmeladha	
jar	το βάζο	to vazo	
jeans	το τζιν	to jean	
jeweller's	το κοσμηματο-	to kosmeemato-	
	πωλείο	poleeo	
jewellery	τα κοσμήματα	ta kosmeemata	
job	η δουλειά	ee dhoolya	
joke	το αστείο	to asteeo	

journey	το ταξίδι	to takseedhee	
juice	ο χυμός	o kheemos	
just: just two	μόνο δύο	mono dheeo	
I've just arrived	μόλις έφτασα	molees eftasa	
K			
to keep	κρατώ	krato	
key	το κλειδί	to kleedhee	
kilo	το κιλό	to keelo	
kilometre	το χιλιόμετρο	to kheelyometro	
kind (sort)	το είδος	to eedhos	
kind adj	ευγενικός	ef-gheneekos	
kiosk	το περίπτερο	to pereeptero	
kitchen	η κουζίνα	ee koozeena	
knife	το μαχαίρι	to makheree	
to knock down	χτυπώ με	khteepo me	
(by car)	αυτοκίνητο	aftokeeneeto	
L			
ladies (toilet)	γυναικών	yeeneekon	

lady	η κυρία	ee keereea
lager	η μπίρα	ee beera
lamb	το αρνάκι	to arnakee
lamp	η λάμπα	ee lamba
to land (plane)	προσγειώνω	prosgheeono
language	η γλώσσα	ee ghlosa
large	μεγάλος	meghalos
last	τελευταίος	telefteos
late (in the day)	αργά	argha
I am late (for an appointment)	έχω αργήσει	ekho argheesee
later	αργότερα	arghotera
lavatory	η τουαλέτα	ee tooaleta
lazy	τεμπέλης	tembelees
to learn	μαθαίνω	matheno
leather	το δέρμα	to dherma
to leave (go away)	φεύγω	fevgho
left: (on/to the) left	αριστερά	areestera

left-luggage (office)	η φύλαξη αποσκευών	ee feelaksee aposkevon
leg	το πόδι	to podhee
lemon	το λεμόνι	to lemonee
lemonade	η λεμονάδα	ee lemonadha
lens	ο φακός	o fakos
less: less milk	λιγότερο γάλα	leeghotero ghala
lesson	το μάθημα	to matheema
to let (allow) (hire out)	επιτρέπω νοικιάζω	epeetrepo neekyazo
letter	το γράμμα	to ghrama
licence	η άδεια	ee adheea
to lie down	ξαπλώνω	ksaplono
lift	το ασανσέρ	to asanser
light	το φως	to fos
to like : I like	μου αρέσει	moo aresee
line	η γραμμή	ee ghramee
to listen	ακούω	akoo-o
litre	το λίτρο	to leetro

English – Greek

English	Greek	Pronunciation
little	μικρός	meekros
a little	λίγο	leegho
to live	μένω	meno
he lives in London	μένει στο Λονδίνο	menee sto londheeno
lock	η κλειδαριά	ee kleedharya
to lock	κλειδώνω	kleedhono
I'm locked out	κλειδώθηκα έξω	kleedhotheeka ekso
London	το Λονδίνο	to londheeno
long	μακρύς	makrees
to look at	κοιτάζω	keetazo
to look after	φροντίζω	frondeezo
to lose	χάνω	khano
lost	χαμένος	khamenos
I've lost my wallet	έχασα το πορτοφόλι μου	ekhasa to portofolee moo
I am lost	χάθηκα	khatheeka

English	Greek	Pronunciation
lost-property office	το γραφείο απωλεσθέντων αντικειμένων	to ghrafeeo apolesthendon andeekeemenon
lot: a lot (of)	πολύς	polees
loud	δυνατός	dheenatos
to love	αγαπώ	aghapo
low	χαμηλός	khameelos
luggage	οι αποσκευές	ee aposkeves
lunch	το μεσημεριανό	to meseemeryano
M		
machine	η μηχανή	ee meekhanee
mad	τρελός	trelos
magazine	το περιοδικό	to pereeodheeko
main course (of meal)	το κύριο πιάτο	to keereeo pyato
to make	κάνω	kano
make-up	το μακιγιάζ	to makeeyaz
male	αρσενικός	arseneekos

English		Greek	
man	o άντρας	o andras	
manager	o διαχειριστής	o dheeakheeree-stees	
many	πολλοί	polee	
many people	πολλοί άνθρωποι	polee anthrope	
map	o χάρτης	o khartees	
market	η αγορά	ee aghora	
married	παντρεμένος	pandremenos	
material	το υλικό	to eeleeko	
matter: it doesn't matter	δεν πειράζει	dhen peerazee	
what's the matter with you?	τι έχεις;	tee ekhees?	
meal	το γεύμα	to yevma	
meat	το κρέας	to kreas	
medicine (drug)	το φάρμακο	to farmako	
Mediterranean	η Μεσόγειος	ee mesoyeeos	
to meet	συναντώ	seenando	

meeting	η συνάντηση	ee seenandeesee	
melon (watermelon)	το πεπόνι	to peponee	
	το καρπούζι	to karpoozee	
men	οι άντρες	ee andres	
menu	o κατάλογος/	o kataloghos/	
	το μενού	to menoo	
message	το μήνυμα	to meeneema	
metre	το μέτρο	to metro	
midday	το μεσημέρι	to meseemeree	
midnight	τα μεσάνυχτα	ta mesaneekhta	
milk	το γάλα	to ghala	
millimetre	το χιλιοστό-μετρο	to kheelyosto-metro	
to mind: do you mind if ...?	σας ενοχλεί αν ...;	sas enokhlee an ...?	
minute	το λεπτό	to lepto	
to miss (train, etc.)	χάνω	khano	
Miss	η Δεσποινίς	ee dhespeenees	
missing	χαμένος	khamenos	
he's missing	λείπει	leepee	

mistake	το λάθος	to lathos	
mobile (phone)	το κινητό (τηλέφωνο)	to keeneeto (teelefono)	
mobile number	ο αριθμός κινητού	o areethmos keeneetoo	
money	τα χρήματα/ τα λεφτά	ta khreemata/ ta lefta	
month	ο μήνας	o meenas	
more	περισσότερο	pereesotero	
more bread	κι άλλο ψωμί	kee alo psomee	
morning	το πρωί	to proee	
most	το περισσότερο	to pereesotero	
mother	η μητέρα	ee metera	
motor	η μηχανή	ee meekhanee	
motorbike	η μοτοσικλέτα	ee motoseekleta	
motorway	ο αυτοκινητό-δρομος	o aftokeeneeto-dhromos	
mouth	το στόμα	to stoma	
to move	κινούμαι	keenoome	
Mr	Κύριος	keereeos	

Mrs	Κυρία	keereea	
much	πολύς	polees	
too much	πάρα πολύ	para polee	
very much	πάρα πολύ	para polee	
museum	το μουσείο	to mooseeo	
music	η μουσική	ee mooseekee	
must: I must go	πρέπει να πάω	prepee na pao	
you must go	πρέπει να πας	prepee na pas	
he/she must go	πρέπει να πάει	prepee na paee	
we must go	πρέπει να πάμε	prepee na pame	

N

name	το όνομα	to onoma	
narrow	στενός	stenos	
nationality	η υπηκοότητα	ee eepeeko-oteeta	
near	κοντά	konda	
necessary	απαραίτητος	apareeteetos	
to need: I need...	χρειάζομαι...	khreeazome...	
never	ποτέ	pote	
new	καινούριος	kenooryos	

English	Greek	pronunciation
news (TV, radio)	οι ειδήσεις	ee eedheesees
newspaper	η εφημερίδα	ee efeemereedha
New Year: happy New Year!	καλή χρονιά!	kalee khronya!
New Zealand	η Νέα Ζηλανδία	ee nea zeeland-heea
next	επόμενος	epomenos
nice (thing)	ωραίος	oreos
(person)	καλός	kalos
night	η νύχτα	ee neekhta
no	όχι	okhee
nobody	κανένας	kanenas
noise	ο θόρυβος	o thoreevos
non-alcoholic	μη οινοπνευματώδης	mee eenopnev-matodhees
none	κανένα	kanena
non-smoking	μη καπνίζοντες	mee kapnee-zondes
north	ο βορράς	o voras
nose	η μύτη	ee meetee
not	μη/ δεν	mee/ dhen
I am not	δεν είμαι	dhen eeme
don't stop	μη σταματάς	mee stamatas
nothing	τίποτα	teepota
now	τώρα	tora
number	ο αριθμός	o areethmos
O		
off (light, machine, etc)	σβηστός	sveestos
it's off (rotten)	είναι χαλασμένο	eene khalasmeno
office	το γραφείο	to ghrafeeo
often	συχνά	seekhna
OK	εντάξει	endaksee
old (person)	ηλικιωμένος	eeleekyomenos
(thing)	παλιός	palyos

English	Greek	Pronunciation
how old are you?	πόσων χρονών είστε;	poson khronon eeste?
on (on top of)	πάνω	pano
on (light, TV)	ανοιχτός	aneekhtos
on the table	(πάνω) στο τραπέζι	(pano) sto trapezee
once	μία φορά	meea fora
only	μόνο	mono
to open	ανοίγω	aneegho
open adj	ανοιχτός	aneektos
opposite	απέναντι	apenandee
or	ή	ee
to order	παραγγέλλω	parang-elo
Orthodox (religion)	ορθόδοξος	orthodhoksos
other	άλλος	alos
out (light, etc.)	σβησμένος	sveesmenos
he's out	λείπει	leepee
outside	έξω	ekso
over	πάνω από	pano apo
over there	εκεί πέρα	ekee pera
to owe: you owe me	μου χρωστάς	moo khrostas

P

English	Greek	Pronunciation
package tour	η οργανωμένη εκδρομή	ee orghanomenee ekdhromee
paid	πληρωμένος	pleeromenos
pain	ο πόνος	o ponos
painful	οδυνηρός	odheeneros
it's painful	πονάει	ponae
painting	ο πίνακας	o peenakas
pair	το ζευγάρι	to zevgharee
pan	η κατσαρόλα	ee katsarola
paper	το χαρτί	to khartee
parcel	το δέμα	to dhema
pardon	παρακαλώ	parakalo
I beg your pardon	με συγχωρείτε	me seenkhoreete
parents	οι γονείς	o ghonees
park noun	το πάρκο	to parko

English – Greek

to park (in car)	παρκάρω	parkaro
part	το μέρος	to meros
passenger	ο επιβάτης	o epevatees
passport control	ο έλεγχος διαβατηρίων	o elengkhos dheeavateereeon
pasta	τα ζυμαρικά	ta zeemareeka
to pay	πληρώνω	pleerono
payment	η πληρωμή	ee pleeromee
pen	το στυλό	to steelo
pensioner	ο/η συνταξιούχος	o/ee seendakseeyookhos
pepper (spice)	το πιπέρι	to peeperee
pepper (vegetable)	η πιπεριά	ee peeperya
per: per hour	την ώρα	teen ora
perfect	τέλειος	teleeos
performance	η παράσταση	ee parastasee
perhaps	ίσως	eesos
person	το άτομο	to atomo
petrol	η βενζίνη	ee venzeenee
petrol station	το βενζινάδικο/το πρατήριο βενζίνης	to venzeenadheeko/to prateereeo venzeenees
pharmacist	ο φαρμακοποιός	o farmakopeeos
phonecard	η τηλεκάρτα	ee teelekarta
photocopy	η φωτοτυπία	ee fototeepeea
photograph	η φωτογραφία	ee fotoghrafeea
pie	η πίτα	ee peeta
pillow	το μαξιλάρι	to makseelaree
platform	η αποβάθρα	ee apovathra
to play	παίζω	pezo
please	παρακαλώ	parakalo
pleased	ευχαριστημένος	efkhareesteemenos
police	η αστυνομία	ee asteenomeea
policeman	ο αστυνόμος	o asteenomos
police station	το αστυνομικό τμήμα	to asteenomeeko tmeema

English – Greek

English	Greek	Pronunciation
pool (for swimming)	η πισίνα	ee peeseena
pork	το χοιρινό	to kheereeno
port (harbour)	το λιμάνι	to leemanee
to post (letter)	ταχυδρομώ	takheedhromo
postcard	η καρτποστάλ	ee kartpostal
postcode	ο κωδικός	o kodheekos
post office	το ταχυδρομείο	to takheedhromeeo
pound (money)	η λίρα	ee leera
to prefer	προτιμώ	proteemo
pregnant	έγγυος	engeeos
to prepare	ετοιμάζω	eteemazo
prescription	η συνταγή	ee seendaghee
present (gift)	το δώρο	to dhoro
pretty	ωραίος	oreos
price	η τιμή	ee teemee
price list	ο τιμοκατά- λογος	o teemokata-loghos
private	ιδιωτικός	eedheeoteekos
problem	το πρόβλημα	to provleema
prohibited	απαγορευ-μένος	apaghorevmenos
to pronounce	προφέρω	profero
how do you pronounce this?	πώς το προφέρετε;	pos to proferete?
public	δημόσιος	dheemoseeos
public holiday	η γιορτή	ee yortee
purse	το πορτοφόλι	to portofolee
to push	σπρώχνω	sprokhno
to put	βάζω	vazo
to put down	βάζω κάτω	vazo kato

Q

quality	η ποιότητα	ee peeoteeta
question	η ερώτηση	ee eroteesee
queue	η ουρά	ee oora
quick	γρήγορος	ghreeghoros
quickly	γρήγορα	ghreeghora

English	Greek	Pronunciation
quiet	ήσυχος	eeseekhos
R		
radio	το ραδιόφωνο	to radhyofono
railway station	ο σιδηρόδρο- μικός σταθμός	o seedheerodhro- mikos stathmos
rain	η βροχή	ee vrokhee
raining: it's raining	βρέχει	vrekhee
rare	σπάνιος	spanyos
(steak)	μισοψημένος	meesopsemenos
rate	ο ρυθμός	o reethmos
rate of exchange	η ισοτιμία	ee eesoteemea
raw	ωμός	omos
razor	το ξυράφι	to kserafee
to read	διαβάζω	dheeavazo
ready	έτοιμος	eteemos
real	πραγματικός	praghmateekos
receipt	η απόδειξη	ee apodheeksee
reception (desk)	η ρεσεψιόν	ee resepsyon

English	Greek	Pronunciation
to recommend	συνιστώ	seeneesto
red	κόκκινος	kokeenos
reduction	η έκπτωση	ee ekptosee
refund	η επιστροφή	ee epeestrofee
registered (letter)	χρημάτων	khreematon
relations (family)	συστημένο	seestemeno
relax	οι συγγενείς	ee seenghenhes
to relax	ξεκουράζομαι	ksekoorazome
to remember	θυμάμαι	theemame
to rent	νοικιάζω	neekyazo
to repair	επιδιορθώνω	epeedheeorthono
to repeat	επαναλαμβάνω	epanalamvano
reservation	η κράτηση	ee krateesee
to reserve	κρατώ	krato
reserved	κρατημένος	krateemenos
rest	ξεκούραση	ksekoorase
the rest (the others)	οι υπόλοιποι	ee eepoleepee
to rest	ξεκουράζομαι	ksekoorazome
restaurant	το εστιατόριο	to esteeatoreeo

English – Greek

retired	συνταξιούχος	seendaksyookhos	
to return (go back, give back)	επιστρέφω	epeestrefo	
return ticket	το εισιτήριο με επιστροφή	to eeseeteereeo me epeestrofee	
rice	το ρύζι	to reezee	
rich (person, food)	πλούσιος	plooseeos	
right (correct, accurate)	σωστός	sostos	
(on/to the) right	δεξιά	dheksya	
road	ο δρόμος	o dhromos	
road map	ο οδικός χάρτης	o odheekos khartees	
roast	το ψητό	to pseeto	
room (in house, etc.)	το δωμάτιο	to dhomateeo	
(space)	ο χώρος	o khoros	
rosé	ροζέ	roze	
round (shape)	στρογγυλός	strongeelos	

round Greece	γύρω στην Ελλάδα	yeero steen eladha	
to run	τρέχω	trekho	

S

sad	λυπημένος	leepeemenos	
safe adj (harmless) (not dangerous)	αβλαβής	avlavees	
(secure, sure)	ακίνδυνος	akeendheenos	
	ασφαλής	asfalees	
salad	η σαλάτα	ee salata	
salt	το αλάτι	to alatee	
same	ίδιος	eedhyos	
sand	η άμμος	ee amos	
sauce	η σάλτσα	ee saltsa	
to say	λέω	leo	
Scotland	η Σκωτία	ee skoteea	
Scottish (person)	ο Σκωτσέζος/ η Σκωτσέζα	o skotsezos/ ee skotseza	
sculpture	το γλυπτό	to ghleepto	
sea	η θάλασσα	ee thalasa	

English	Greek	Pronunciation
seafood	τα θαλασσινά	ta thalaseena
seaside (beach, seafront)	η παραλία	ee paraleea
seat (in theatre)	η θέση	ee thesee
seat (in car, etc.)	το κάθισμα	to katheesma
second	δεύτερος	dhefteros
to see	βλέπω	vlepo
to sell	πουλώ	poolo
send	στέλνω	stelno
to serve	σερβίρω	serveero
service (in restaurant, etc.)	η εξυπηρέτηση	ee ekseepeereeteesee
shallow	ρηχός	reekhos
shampoo	το σαμπουάν	to sambooan
to share	μοιράζω	meerazo
shaver	η ξυριστική μηχανή	ee kseereesteekee meekhanee
she	αυτή	aftee
sheet	το σεντόνι	to sendonee
ship	το πλοίο	to pleeo
shirt	το πουκάμισο	to pookameeso
shoe	το παπούτσι	to papootsee
to shop	ψωνίζω	psoneezo
shop	το μαγαζί	to maghazee
short	κοντός	kondos
show (in theatre, etc.)	η παράσταση	ee parastasee
to show	δείχνω	dheekhno
shower (in bath)	το ντους	to doos
(rain)	η μπόρα	ee bora
shut (closed)	κλειστός	kleestos
to shut	κλείνω	kleeno
sick (ill)	άρρωστος	arostos
to be sick (vomit)	κάνω εμετό	kano emeto
sign (roadsign, notice, etc.)	η πινακίδα	ee peenakeedha
signature	η υπογραφή	ee eepoghrafee
silver	ασημένιος	aseemenyos
to sing	τραγουδώ	traghoodho
single (not married)	ελεύθερος	eleftheros

English – Greek

English – Greek

single bed	το μονό κρεβάτι	to mono krevatee	soap	το σαπούνι	to sapoonee
single room	το μονόκλινο δωμάτιο	to monokleeno dhomateeo	soft drink	το αναψυκτικό	to anapseekteeko
sister	η αδελφή	ee adhelfee	some	μερικοί	mereekee
to sit (down)	κάθομαι	kathome	someone	κάποιος	kapyos
size (of clothes, shoes)	το νούμερο	to noomero	something	κάτι	katee
			sometimes	κάποτε	kapote
skin	το δέρμα	to dherma	son	ο γιος	o yos
skirt	η φούστα	ee foosta	song	το τραγούδι	to traghoodhee
sky	ο ουρανός	o ooranos	soon	σύντομα	seendoma
to sleep	κοιμούμαι	keemoome	as soon as possible	το συντομότερο	to seendomotero
slice	η φέτα	ee feta	sooner	νωρίτερα	noretera
slow	σιγά	seegha	sorry: I'm sorry (apology)	συγγνώμη	seeghnomee
small	μικρός	meekros			
smell	η μυρωδιά	ee meerodhya	soup	η σούπα	ee soopa
smile	το χαμόγελο	to khamoyelo	south	ο νότος	o notos
to smile	χαμογελώ	khamoyelo	to speak	μιλώ	meelo
smoke	ο καπνός	o kapnos	special	ειδικός	eedheekos
to smoke	καπνίζω	kapneezo	special needs	ειδικές ανάγκες	eedheekes anangkes
snow	το χιόνι	to khyonee			

English	Greek	
speed	η ταχύτητα	ee takheeteeta
speed limit	το όριο ταχύτητας	to oreeo takheeteetas
spirits	τα οινοπνευματώδη ποτά	ta eenopnevmatodhee pota
spoon	το κουτάλι	to kootalee
sport	το σπορ	to spor
spring (season)	η άνοιξη	ee aneeksee
square (in town)	η πλατεία	ee plateea
stamp	το γραμματόσημο	to ghramatoseemo
to start	αρχίζω	arkheezo
starter (in meal)	το ορεκτικό	to orekteeko
station	ο σταθμός	o stathmos
to stay	μένω	meno
steak	η μπριζόλα	ee breezola
sterling	η αγγλική λίρα	ee angleekee leera
still (yet) **(immobile)** **(water)**	ακόμα ακίνητος μη αεριούχο	akoma akeeneetos mee aereeookho
to stop	σταματώ	stamato
straight: **straight on**	ευθεία	eftheea
strawberry	η φράουλα	ee fraoola
street	ο δρόμος	o dhromos
street plan	ο οδικός χάρτης	o odheekos khartees
strong	δυνατός	dheenatos
student	ο φοιτητής/ η φοιτήτρια	o feeteetees/ ee feeteetreea
sugar	η ζάχαρη	ee zakharee
suitcase	η βαλίτσα	ee valeetsa
summer	το καλοκαίρι	to kalokeree
sun	ο ήλιος	o eeleeos
to sunbathe	κάνω ηλιοθεραπεία	kano eeleeotherapeea

English – Greek

English - Greek

sunburn (painful)	το κάψιμο από τον ήλιο	to kapseemo apo ton eeleeo
suncream	η αντηλιακή κρέμα	ee andee-eeleeakee krema
sunglasses	τα γυαλιά του ήλιου	ta yalya too eeleeoo
sunny (weather)	ηλιόλουστος	eeleeoloostos
sunrise	η ανατολή	ee anatolee
sunset	το ηλιοβασίλεμα	to eeleeovasee-lema
sunshade	η ομπρέλα	ee ombrela
supermarket	το σούπερ-μάρκετ	to supermarket
supper	το δείπνο	to dheepno
surfing	το σέρφινγκ	to serfeeng
surname	το επώνυμο	to eponeemo
to sweat	ιδρώνω	eedhrono
sweater	το πουλόβερ	to poolover
sweet (dessert)	το γλυκό	to ghleeko
to swim	κολυμπώ	koleembo

swimming pool	η πισίνα	ee peeseena
swimsuit	το μαγιό	to mayo
to switch on	ανάβω	anavo
to switch off	σβήνω	sveeno
swollen (ankle, etc.)	πρησμένος	preesmenos

T

table	το τραπέζι	to trapezee
tablet	το χάπι	to khapee
to take out (from bank account)	παίρνω	perno
to talk	βγάζω	vghazo
	αποσύρω	aposeero
	μιλώ	meelo
tall	ψηλός	pseelos
to taste	δοκιμάζω	dhokeemazo
taste noun	η γεύση	ee yefsee
taxi	το ταξί	to taksee
tea	το τσάι	to tsaee
to teach	διδάσκω	dheedhasko

English	Greek	Pronunciation
teacher	ο δάσκαλος/ η δασκάλα	o dhaskalos/ ee dhaskala
teeth	τα δόντια	ta dhondya
telephone	το τηλέφωνο	to teelefono
telephone call	το τηλεφώνημα	to teelefoneema
television	η τηλεόραση	ee teeleorasee
to tell (story)	λέγω διηγούμαι	legho dhee-eeghoome
temperature	η θερμοκρασία	ee thermokraseea
to have a temperature	έχω πυρετό	ekho peereto
temporary	προσωρινός	prosoreenos
tennis	το τένις	to tenees
tent	η σκηνή	ee skenee
to text	θα σου στείλω μήνυμα	tha soo steelo meeneema
I'll text you	μήνυμα	meeneema
thank you	ευχαριστώ	efkhareesto
that	εκείνος	ekenos
that book	εκείνο το βιβλίο	ekeeno to veevleeo
that one	εκείνο	ekeeno
theatre	το θέατρο	to theatro
then	τότε	tote
there	εκεί	ekee
there is	υπάρχει	eeparkhee
there are	υπάρχουν	eeparkhoon
these (feminine) (masculine) (neuter)	αυτοί/ αυτές/ αυτά	afta/ aftee/ aftes
these books	αυτά τα βιβλία	afta ta veevleea
they	αυτοί	aftee
thief	ο κλέφτης	o kleftees
thing	το πράγμα	to praghma
thirsty: I'm thirsty	διψάω	dheepsao
this (masculine) (feminine) (neuter)	αυτός/ αυτή/ αυτό	aftos/ aftee/ afto
this book	αυτό το βιβλίο	afto to veevleeo
this one	αυτό	afto

those	εκείνοι	ekeenee
those books	εκείνα τα βιβλία	ekeena ta veevleea
through	διαμέσου	dheeameesoo
ticket	το εισιτήριο	to eeseeteereeo
tie	η γραβάτα	ee ghravata
till (cash)	το ταμείο	to tameeo
till (until)	μέχρι	mekhree
time (by the clock)	η ώρα	ee ora
what time is it?	τι ώρα είναι;	tee ora eene?
timetable (buses, trains, etc)	το δρομολόγιο	to dromoloyeeo
timetable (school, shop opening hours etc)	το ωράριο	to orareeo
tip (to water, etc)	το πουρμπουάρ	to poorbooar
tired	κουρασμένος	koorasmenos
tissue	το χαρτομάντηλο	to khartomandeelo
to	σε	se
to the (masculine)	στο/	sto/
(feminine)	στη/	stee/
(neuter)	στο	sto
to Greece	στην Ελλάδα	steen eladha
tobacco	ο καπνός	o kapnos
together	μαζί	mazee
toilet	η τουαλέτα	ee tooaleta
toilet paper	το χαρτί υγείας	to khartee eeyeeas
toll	τα διόδια	ta dheeodheea
tomato	η ντομάτα	ee domata
tomorrow	αύριο	avreeo
tonight	απόψε	apopse
too (also)	επίσης	epeesees
(too much)	πάρα πολύ	para polee
tooth	το δόντι	to dhondee
toothache	ο πονόδοντος	o ponodhondos
toothbrush	η οδοντόβουρτσα	ee odhonto-voortsa
toothpaste	η οδοντόκρεμα	ee odhondokrema

top		
(of mountain)	το πάνω μέρος	to pano meros
	η κορυφή	ee koreefee
total	το σύνολο	to seenolo
tour	η εκδρομή	ee ekdhromee
tourist	ο τουρίστας/	o tooreestas/
	η τουρίστρια	ee tooreestrea
tourist office	το τουριστικό	to tooreesteeko
	γραφείο	ghrafeeo
town	η πόλη	ee polee
town centre	το κέντρο της	to kendro tees
	πόλης	polees
town plan	ο χάρτης της	o khartees tees
	πόλης	polees
toy	το παιχνίδι	to pekhneedhee
traditional	παραδοσιακός	paradhoseeakos
traffic	η κυκλοφορία	ee keekloforeea
traffic lights	τα φανάρια	ta fanarya
	(της τροχαίας)	(trees trokheas)
train	το τρένο	to treno
to translate	μεταφράζω	metafrazo

to travel	ταξιδεύω	takseedhevo
travel agent	ο ταξιδιωτικός	o takseedhyotee-
	πράκτορας	kos praktoras
travellers' cheques	τα ταξιδιωτικά	ta takseedhyo-
	τσεκ	teeka tsek
tree	το δέντρο	to dhendro
trip	η εκδρομή	ee ekdhromee
trouble	ο μπελάς	o belas
trousers	το παντελόνι	to pandelonee
true	αληθινός	aleetheenos
to try	προσπαθώ	prospatho
to try on	δοκιμάζω	dhokeemazo
T-shirt	το μπλουζάκι	to bloozakee
to turn off	στρίβω	streevo
(on a journey)	στρίβω	streevo
(radio, etc.)	κλείνω	kleeno
(engine, light)	σβήνω	sveeno

English – Greek

to turn on (radio, TV) (engine, light)	ανοίγω	aneegho
	ανάβω	anavo
TV	η τηλεόραση	ee teeleorase
twice	δύο φορές	dheeo fores
twin-bedded	το δίκλινο δωμάτιο	to dheekleeno dhomateeo
U		
ugly	άσχημος	askheemos
umbrella	η ομπρέλα	ee ombrela
uncle	ο θείος	o theeos
under	άβολος	avolos
underground (railway)	κάτω από	kato apo
	το μετρό	to metro
to understand	καταλαβαίνω	katalaveno
underwear	τα εσώρουχα	ta esoorookha
unemployed	άνεργος	anerghos

United States	οι Ηνωμένες Πολιτείες	ee eenomenes poleeteeyes
university	το πανεπιστήμιο	to panepeesteemeeo
until	μέχρι/ έως	mekhree/ eos
upstairs	πάνω	pano
urgently	επειγόντως	epeeghondos
to use	χρησιμοποιώ	khreeseemopeeo
useful	χρήσιμος	khreeseemos
usually	συνήθως	seeneethos
V		
vacancy (room)	το διαθέσιμο δωμάτιο	to dheeatheseemo dhomateeo
valuable	πολύτιμος	poleeteemos
value	η αξία	ee akseea
VAT	ο ΦΠΑ	o fee pee a
vegetables	τα λαχανικά	ta lakhaneeka
vegetarian	ο χορτοφάγος	o khortofaghos

English	Greek	
very	πολύ	polee
video	το βίντεο	to veedeo
view	η θέα	ee thea
villa	η βίλλα	ee veela
village	το χωριό	to khoryo
visa	η βίζα	ee veesa
to visit	επισκέπτομαι	epeeskeptome
visit	επίσκεψη	ee epeeskepsee
voice	η φωνή	ee fonee

W

to wait for	περιμένω	pereemeno
waiter	το γκαρσόνι	to garsonee
waiting room	η αίθουσα αναμονής	ee ethoosa anamonees
waitress	η σερβιτόρα	ee serveetora
Wales	η Ουαλία	ee ooalea
walk	ο περίπατος	o pereepatos
to walk	περπατώ	perpato
wall	ο τοίχος	o teekhos

wallet	το πορτοφόλι	to portofolee
to want	θέλω	thelo
warm	ζεστός	zestos
to wash (clothes)	πλένω	pleno
(oneself)	πλένομαι	plenome
watch noun	το ρολόι	to roloee
to watch (TV)	βλέπω	vlepo
(someone's luggage)	προσέχω	prosekho
water	το νερό	to nero
watermelon	το καρπούζι	to karpoozee
way (method)	ο τρόπος	o tropos
this way	από 'δω	apodho
that way	από 'κει	apokee
we	εμείς	emees
weak	αδύνατος	adheenatos
to wear	φορώ	foro
weather	ο καιρός	o keros
wedding	ο γάμος	o ghamos
week	η εβδομάδα	ee evdhomadha

English – Greek

English	Greek	Pronunciation
weekend	το σαββατοκύ- ριακο	to savatokeeryako
weekly (rate, etc.)	εβδομαδιαιος	evdhomadhee-eos
weight	το βάρος	to varos
welcome	καλώς ήλθατε	kalos eelthate
well (healthy)	καλά	kala
Welsh (person)	ο Ουαλός/ η Ουαλή	o ooalos/ ee ooalee
west	η δύση	ee dheese
what	τι	tee
what is it?	τι είναι;	tee eene?
wheelchair	η αναπηρική καρέκλα	ee anapeereekee karekla
when?	πότε;	pote?
where?	πού;	poo?
which? (masculine)	ποιος;	pyos?
(feminine)	ποια;	pya?
(neuter)	ποιο;	pyo?
which is it?	ποιο είναι;	pyo eene?
while	ενώ	eno
white	άσπρος	aspros
who?	ποιος;	pyos?
whole	όλος	olos
whose: whose is it?	ποιανού είναι;	pyanoo eene?
why?	γιατί;	yatee?
wide	πλατύς	platees
wife	η σύζυγος	ee seezeeghos
wind	ο αέρας	o a-eras
window	το παράθυρο	to paratheero
wine	το κρασί	to krasee
winter	ο χειμώνας	o kheemonas
with	με	me
without	χωρίς	khorees
woman	η γυναίκα	ee yeeneka
word	η λέξη	ee leksee
work	η δουλειά	ee dhoolya
to work (person)	δουλεύω	dhoolevo
(machine)	λειτουργεί	leetoorghee

worried	ανήσυχος	aneeseekhos
to write	γράφω	ghrafo
wrong	λάθος	lathos
you're wrong	κάνετε λάθος	kanete lathos

Y

year	ο χρόνος	o khronos
yellow	κίτρινος	keetreenos
yes	ναι	ne
yesterday	χτες	khtes
yet	ακόμα	akoma
not yet	όχι ακόμα	okhee akoma
yoghurt	το γιαούρτι	to yaoortee
you (singular/ plural)	εσύ/ εσείς	esee/ esees
young	νέος	neos
youth hostel	ο ξενώνας	o ksenonas
	νεότητος	neoteetos

Z

| zero | το μηδέν | to meedhen |
| zone | η ζώνη | ee zonee |

Greek – English

αΑ

Greek	Pronunciation	English
άγαλμα (το)	aghalma	statue
αγάπη (η)	aghapee	love
αγαπώ	aghapo	to love
Αγγλία (η)	angleea	England
αγγλικός/ή/ό	angleekos/ee/o	English (thing)
Άγγλος/ Αγγλίδα (ο/η)	anglos/ angleedha	Englishman/ -woman
άγιος/α/ο	agheeos/a/o	holy, saint
Άγιον Όρος (το)	agheeon oros	Mount Athos
αγορά (η)	aghora	market
αγοράζω	aghorazo	to buy
αγόρι (το)	aghoree	young boy
άδεια (η)	adheea	permit, licence
άδεια	adheea	driving licence
οδήγησης	odheegheesees	
άδειος/α/ο	adheeos/a/o	empty
αδελφή (η)	adhelfee	sister
αδελφός (ο)	adhelfos	brother

Greek	Pronunciation	English
αδίκημα (το)	adheekeema	offence
αέρας (ο)	aeras	wind
αεροδρόμιο (το)	aerodhromeeo	airport
αεροπλάνο (το)	aeroplano	aeroplane
αεροπορικό εισιτήριο (το)	aeroporeeko eeseeteereeo	air ticket
Αθήνα (η)	atheena	Athens
αθλητικό κέντρο (το)	athleeteeko kendro	sports centre
αθλητισμός (ο)	athleeteesmos	sports
Αιγαίο (το)	egheo	the Aegean Sea
αίμα (το)	ema	blood
αίτηση (η)	eteesee	application
ακούω	akoo-o	to hear
Ακρόπολη (η)	akropolee	the Acropolis
ακτή (η)	aktee	beach, shore
αλάτι (το)	alatee	salt
αλλαγή (η)	alaghee	change

Greek – English

Greek	Pronunciation	English
αλλάζω	alazo	to change
αμάξι (το)	amaksee	car, vehicle
αμερικάνικος/η/ο	amereekaneekos/ee/o	American (thing)
Αμερικάνος/ Αμερικανίδα (η)	amereekaneedha	American (man/woman)
Αμερική (η)	amereekee	America
αμέσως	amesos	at once, immediately
άμμος (η)	amos	sand
αν	an	if
ανάβω	anavo	to switch on
αίθουσα αναμονής (η)	ethoosa anamonees	waiting room
ανάπηρος/ η/ο	anapeeros/ee/o	handicapped, disabled
ανατολή (η)	anatolee	east, sunrise
ανατολικός/ ή/ό	anatoleekos/ee/o	eastern
αναψυκτικό (το)	anapseekteeko	soft drink
άνδρας (ο)	andhras	man, male
ανθοπωλείο (το)	anthopoleo	florist's
άνθρωπος (ο)	anthropos	person
ανοίγω	aneegho	to open
άνοιξη (η)	aneeksee	spring (season)
ανταλλαγή (η)	andalaghee	exchange
αντιβιοτικά (το)	andeeveeoteeka	antibiotics
αντίγραφο (το)	andeeghrafo	copy
αντίκες (οι)	aneekes	antiques
αντίο	andeo	goodbye
απαγορεύω	apaghorevo	to forbid: no...
απάντηση (η)	apanteesee	answer
απέναντι	apenandee	opposite
απογείωση (η)	apogeeosee	takeoff
απόγευμα (το)	apoyevma	afternoon
απόδειξη (η)	apodheeksee	receipt

Greek - English

Greek	Pronunciation	English
αποσκευές (οι)	aposkeves	luggage
αναζήτηση αποσκευών	anazeeteesee aposkevon	left-luggage (office)
απόψε	apopse	tonight
αργότερα	arghotera	later
αρέσω	areso	to please
μου αρέσει	moo aresee	I like
δεν μου αρέσει	dhen moo aresee	I don't like
σου αρέσει	soo aresee	you like
δεν σου αρέσει	dhen soo aresee	you don't like
αριθμός (ο)	areethmos	number
αριθμός τηλεφώνου	areethmos teelefonoo	telephone number
αριστερά	areestera	left (opposite of right)
αρνί (το)	arnee	lamb
αρρώστια (η)	arosteea	illness
άρρωστος/η/ο	arostos/ee/o	ill
αρχαίος/α/ο	arkheos/a/o	ancient
αρχή (η)	arkhee	start, beginning
αρχίζω	arkheezo	to begin, to start
άρωμα (το)	aroma	perfume
ασανσέρ (το)	asanser	lift, elevator
ασθενής (ο/η)	asthenees	patient
ασπιρίνη (η)	aspeereenee	aspirin
άσπρος/η/ο	aspros/ee/o	white
αστυνομία (η)	asteenomeea	police
αστυνομία αλλοδαπών	asteenomeea alodhapon	immigration police
αστυνομία Ελληνική	asteenomeea eleneekee	Greek police
αστυνομικό τμήμα (το)	asteenomeeko tmeema	police station
αστυνομικός σταθμός (ο)	asteenomeekos stathmos	police station
αστυνόμος (ο)	asteenomos	policeman
ασφάλεια (η)	asfaleea	insurance, fuse
ιατρική ασφάλιση	eeatreekee asfaleesee	medical insurance
άτομο (το)	atomo	person

αα		
ατύχημα (το)	ateekheema	accident
αυτοκίνητο (το)	aftokeeneeto	car
ενοικιάσεις αυτοκινήτων	eneekyasees aftokeeneeton	car hire
αυτοκινήτων συνεργείο	aftokeeneeton seenergheeon	car repairs
αυτοκινητό-δρομος (ο)	aftokeeneeto-dhromos	motorway
αυτόματος/η/ο	aftomatos/ee/o	automatic
άφιξη (η)	afeeksee	arrival
ββ		
βαγόνι (το)	vaghonee	carriage (train)
βάζω	vazo	to put
βαλίτσα (η)	valeetsa	suitcase
βαρέλι: μπύρα από βαρέλι	beera apo varelee	draught beer

βαρελίσιο κρασί (το)	vareleeseeo krasee	house wine
βάρκα (η)	varka	boat
βάρος (το)	varos	weight
βγάζω	vghazo	to take off
βγαίνω	vgheno	to go out
βενζίνη (η)	venzeenee	petrol, gasoline
βήχας (ο)	veekhas	cough
βιβλίο (το)	veevleeo	book
βιβλιοπωλείο (το)	veevleeopoleeo	bookshop
βλέπω	vlepo	to see
βοήθεια (η)	voeetheea	help
οδική βοήθεια	odheekee voeetheea	breakdown service
πρώτες βοήθειες	protes voeethee-es	casualty (hospital)
βόλτα (η)	volta	walk, drive, trip
Βόρειος/α/ο	voreeos/a/o	northern
βορράς (ο)	voras	north

Greek - English

Greek		
βουνό (το)	voono	mountain
βράδυ (το)	vradhee	evening
βραδινό (το)	vradheeno	evening meal
βράζω	vrazo	to boil
Βρετανία (η)	vretaneea	Britain
Βρετανός/ Βρετανίδα (ο/η)	vretanos/ vretaneedha	British (man/woman)
βρίσκω	vreesko	to find
βρόμικος/η/ο	vromeekos/ee/o	dirty
βροχή (η)	vrokhee	rain
ΥΓ		
γάλα (το)	ghala	milk
γαλάζιος/α/ο	ghalazeeos/a/o	blue, light blue
γάμος (ο)	ghamos	wedding, marriage
γειά σας	ya sas	hello, goodbye (formal)
γειά σου	ya soo	hello, goodbye (informal)
γεμάτος/η/ο	yematos/ee/o	full
γενέθλια (τα)	yenetheea	birthday
γενικός/ή/ό	yeneekos/ee/o	general
γέννηση (η)	yeneesee	birth
γεύμα (το)	yevma	meal
γέφυρα (η)	yefeera	bridge
για	ya	for
γιαγιά (η)	yaya	grandmother
γιατί;	yatee?	why?
γιατρός (ο/η)	yatros	doctor
γιορτή (η)	yortee	festival, celebration, name day
γιος (ο)	yos	son
γκάζι (το)	gazee	accelerator (car), gas
γκαλερί	galeree	art gallery, art sales

Greek	Pronunciation	English
γκαράζ (το)	garaz	garage
γκαρσόν (το)/ γκαρσόνι/ο / γκαρσόνι (τα)	garson/garsonee	waiter
γλυκός/ιά/ό	gleekos/ya/o	sweet
γλυκά (τα)	gleeko/gheeka	cakes and pastries, desserts
γλυπτική (η)	gleepteekee	sculpture
γλώσσα (η)	ghlosa	tongue, language, sole (fish)
γονείς (οι)	ghonees	parents
γράμμα (το)	ghrama	letter
γράμμα κατεπείγον	ghrama katepeeghon	express letter
γράμμα συστημένο	ghrama seesteemeno	recorded delivery
γραμμάριο (το)	ghramareeo	gram
γραμματοκι-βώτιο (το)	ghramatokeevo-teeo	letter box

Greek	Pronunciation	English
Γραμματό-σημο (το)	ghramatoseemo	stamp
Γραφείο (το)	ghrafeeo	office, desk
Γραφείο Τουρισμού	ghrafeeo tooreesmoo	Tourist Office
Γράφω	ghrafo	to write
Γρήγορα	ghreegora	quickly
Γρίπη (η)	ghreepee	influenza
Γυαλί (το)	yalee	glass
Γυαλιά (τα)	yalya	glasses
Γυαλιά ηλίου	yalya eeleeoo	sunglasses
Γυμναστήριο (το)	yeemnasteereeo	gym

δΔ

Greek	Pronunciation	English
Γυναίκα (η)	yeeneka	woman
Γύρω	yeero	round, about
Γωνία (η)	ghonea	corner
δάσος (το)	dhasos	forest, wood
δείπνο (το)	dheepno	dinner

Greek – English

Greek – English

δέκα	dheka	ten	
Δελφοί (οι)	dhelfee	Delphi	
δεν	dhen	not	
δεξιά	dhekseea	right (opposite of left)	
δέρμα (το)	dherma	skin, leather	
δεσποινίς/	dhespeenees/	Miss	
δεσποινίδα (η)	dhespeeneedha		
δεύτερος/η/ο	dhefteros/ee/o	second	
δήλωση (η)	dheelosee	announcement	
είδη προς	eedhee pros	goods to declare	
δήλωση	dheelosee		
ουδέν προς	oodhen pros	nothing to	
δήλωση	dheelosee	declare	
δημαρχείο (το)	dheemarkheeo	town hall	
δημόσιος/α/ο	dheemoseeos	public/state	
δημόσια έργα	dheemoseea ergha	road works	
δημόσιος	dheemoseeos	public gardens	
κήπος	keepos		
δημοτικός/ή/ό	deemoteekos	public/municipal	
Δημοτική	dheemoteekee	public market	
Αγορά	aghora		
διάβαση (η)	dheeavasee	crossing	
διαβατήριο	dheeavateereeo	passport	
(το)			
διαβήτης (ο)	dheeaveetees	diabetes	
διαδρομή (η)	dheeadhromee	route	
διακεκριμένη	dheeakekree-	business class	
θέση	menee thesee		
διακοπές (οι)	dheeakopes	holidays	
διάλειμμα (το)	dheealeema	interval, break	
διαμέρισμα	dheeamereesma	flat, apartment	
(το)			
διανυχτερεύει	dheeaneekhterevee	open all night	
διασκέδαση (η)	dheeaskedhasee	entertainment	
κέντρο διασ–	kendro	nightclub	
κέδασεως	dheeaskedaseos		
διασταύρωση	dheeastavrosee	crossroads,	
(η)		junction	

Greek	Pronunciation	English
διεθνής/ής/ές	dhee-ethnees/ees/es	international
διεύθυνση (η)	dhee-eftheensee	address
διευθυντής (ο)	dhee-eftheentees	manager
δικαστήριο (το)	dheekasteereeo	court
δικηγόρος (ο/η)	dheekeeghoros	lawyer
δίνω	dheeno	to give
διπλά	dheepla	next to
διπλός/ή/ό	dheeplos/ee/o	double
διπλό δωμάτιο	dheeplodomateeo	double room
διπλό κρεβάτι	dheeplo krevatee	double bed
δολάριο (το)	dholareeo	dollar
δόντι (το)	dhondee	tooth
δρομολόγιο (το)	dhromologheeo	timetable, route
δρόμος (ο)	dhromos	street, way
δύση (η)	dheese	west, sunset
δύσκολος/η/ο	dheeskolos/ee/o	difficult
δυστύχημα (το)	dheesteekheema	accident, mishap
δυτικός/ή/ό	dheetikos/ee/o	western
Δωδεκάνησα (τα)	dhodhekaneesa	the Dodecanese
δωμάτιο (το)	dhomateeo	room
δωρεάν	dhorean	free of charge
δώρο (το)	dhoro	present, gift

εΕ

εβδομάδα (η)	evdhomadha	week
εγγύηση (η)	engheeyeesee	guarantee
εδώ	edho	here
εθνικός/ή/ό	ethneekos/ee/o	national
Εθνικό Θέατρο	ethneeko theatro	National Theatre
εθνική οδός	ethneekee odhos	motorway
έθνος (το)	ethnos	nation
εθνικότητα	ethneekoteeta	nationality
ειδικός/ή/ό	eedheekos/ee/o	special, specialist
είδος (το)	eedhos	kind, sort
είδη	eedhee	goods

Greek - English

Greek	Pronunciation	English
είμαι	eeme	to be
εισιτήριο (το)	eeseeteereeo	ticket
εκδόσεις	ekdhoses	ticket office
εισιτηρίων	eeseeteereeon	ticket office
εκεί	ekee	there
έκθεση (η)	ekthesee	exhibition
εκκλησία (η)	ekleesea	church, chapel
έκπτωση (η)	ekptosee	discount
εκτελούνται έργα	ekteloonde ergha	road works
εκτός	ektos	except, unless
εκτός	ektos	out of order
λειτουργίας	leetoorgheeas	
έλα!	ela!	come on! (singular)
ελάτε!	elate!	come on! (plural)
ελαιόλαδο (το)	eleoladho	olive oil
ελαττώνω	elatono	to reduce, to decrease
ελαττώσατε ταχύτητα	elatosate takheeteeta	reduce speed
έλεγχος (ο)	elenkhos	control
έλεγχος διαβατηρίων	elenkhos dheeavateereeon	passport control
έλεγχος εισιτηρίων	elenkhos eeseeteereeon	check-in
ελεύθερος/η/ο	eleftheros/ee/o	single, free
ελιά (η)	elya	olive, olive tree
Ελλάδα (η)	eladha	Greece
Έλληνας/ Ελληνίδα (η)	elenas/ eleeneedha	Greek (man/woman)
ελληνικά (τα)	eleeneeka	Greek (language)
ελληνικός/η/ό	eleeneekos/ee/o	Greek (thing)
εμπρός	embros	forward, in front, 'hello!' (on phone)
ένας/μία/ένα	enas/meea/ena	one
ενήλικος (ο)	eneeleekos	adult

Greek	Transliteration	English
εννέα/εννιά	enea/enya	nine
ενοικιάζω	eneekeeazo	to rent, to hire
ενοικιάζεται	eneekeeazete	to let
ενοικιάσεις	eneekeeasees	for hire
ενοίκιο (το)	eneekeeo	rent
εντάξει	endaksee	all right, OK
έντυπο (το)	endeepo	form (to fill in)
έξι	eksee	six
εξυπηρέτηση (η)	ekseepeereeteesee	service
έξω	ekso	out, outside
εξωτερικός: το εξωτερικό	to eksotereeko	abroad
ΕΟΤ	e-ot	Greek Tourist Organisation
επάγγελμα (το)	epanghelma	occupation, profession
επείγον/επείγουσα	epeeghon/epeeghoosa	urgent, express
επείγοντα	epeeghonta	casualty
περιστατικά	pereestateeka	department
επιβάτης/τρια (ο/η)	epevatees/treea	passenger
επιβεβαιώνω	epeeveveono	to confirm
επιβίβαση (n)	epeeveevasee	boarding
κάρτα	karta	boarding card
επιβιβάσεως	epeeveevaseos	
επειδή	epeedhee	because
επιδόρπιο (το)	epeedhorpeeo	dessert
επικίνδυνος/ η/ο	epeekeendeenos/ ee/o	dangerous
επίσης	epeesees	also, the same to you
επισκέπτης (ο)	epeeskeptees	visitor
επίσκεψη (η)	epeeskepsee	visit
επιστροφή (η)	epeestrofee	return, return ticket
επιστροφές	epeestrofes	returned goods, refunds
επιταγή (η)	epeetaghee	cheque, invoice

Greek - English

Greek	Pronunciation	English
επόμενος/η/ο	epomenos/ee/o	next
εποχή (η)	epokhee	season
επτά / εφτά	epta/efta	seven
Επτάνησα (τα)	eptaneesa	Ionian Islands
επώνυμο (το)	eponeemo	surname, last name
έργα (τα)	ergha	works
έργο	ergho	film, play, TV program
εργοστάσιο (το)	erghostaseeo	factory
έρχομαι	erkhome	to come
ερώτηση (η)	eroteesee	question
εστιατόριο (το)	esteeatoreeo	restaurant
εσώρουχα (τα)	esorookha	underwear, lingerie
εσωτερικός· πτήσεις εσωτερικού	pteesees esotereekoo	domestic flights
έτος (το)	etos	year
έτσι	etsee	so, like this
ευθεία (η)	eftheea	straight
ευθύνη (η)	eftheenee	responsibility
ευκαιρία (η)	efkereea	opportunity, bargain
εύκολος/η/ο	efkolos/ee/o	easy
Ευρωπαϊκή Ένωση	evropaeekee enosee	European Union
ευρωπαϊκός/ή/ό	evropaeekos/ee/o	European
Ευρώπη (η)	evropee	Europe
ευχαριστώ	efkhareesto	thank you
εφημερίδα (η)	efeemereedha	newspaper
έχω	ekho	to have

Ζζ

ζάλη (η)	zalee	dizziness
ζαμπόν (το)	zambon	ham
ζάχαρη (η)	zakharee	sugar

ζαχαρο- πλαστείο (το)	zakharoplasteeo	patisserie
ζέστη (η)	zestee	heat
κάνει ζέστη	kanee zestee	it's hot
ζευγάρι (το)	zevgharee	couple
ζημιά (η)	zeemya	damage
ζητώ	zeeto	to ask, to seek
ζυμαρικά (τα)	zeemareekha	pasta products
ζωγραφιά (η)	zoghrafya	picture, painting
ζώνη (η)	zonee	belt
ζώνη ασφαλείας	zonee asfaleeas	safety belt, seat belt
ζώο (το)	zo-o	animal

ηΗ

η	ee	the (with feminine nouns)
ή	ee	or
ηλεκτρικός/ή/ό	eelektreekos/ee/o	electrical

ηλεκτρισμός (ο)	eelektreesmos	electricity
ηλεκτρονικός/ή/ό	eelektroneekos/ee/o	electronic
ηλίαση (η)	eeleeasee	sunstroke
ηλικία (η)	eeleekeea	age
ηλιοβασίλεμα (το)	eeleeovaseelema	sunset
ηλιοθεραπεία (η)	eeleeotherapeea	sunbathing
ήλιος (ο)	eeleeos	sun
ημέρα (η)	eemera	day
ημερήσιος/α/ο	eemereeseeos/a/o	daily
ημερομηνία λήξης	eemeromeneea leeksees	expiry date
ημιδιατροφή (η)	eemeedheeatrofee	half board
Ηνωμένο Βασίλειο (το)	eenomeno vaseeleeo	United Kingdom (UK)

Greek – English

Greek - English

Ηνωμένες Πολιτείες της Αμερικής	eenomenes poleetee-es tees amereekes	United States of America	
ΗΠΑ (n)		USA	
ησυχία (n)	eesekheea	calm, quiet	

ΘΘ

θάλασσα (n)	thalasa	sea	
θαλάσσιο σκι	thalaseeo skee	water-skiing	
θέατρο (το)	theatro	theatre	
θέλω	thelo	to want	
θεός/θεά (ο/n)	theos/thea	god/goddess	
θεραπεία (n)	therapeea	treatment	
θέρμανση (n)	thermansee	heating	
θέση (n)	thesee	place, seat	
κράτηση *θέσης*	krateesee thesees	seat reservation	
οικονομική *θέση*	eekonomeekee thesee	economy class	
πρώτη θέση	protee thesee	first class	

Θεσσαλονίκη (n)	thesaloneekee		Salonica/ Thessaloniki
θύρα (n)	theera		gate (airport)
θυρίδα (n)	theereedha		ticket window

ΙΙ

ιατρική περίθαλψη (n)	eeatreekee pereethalpsee		medical treatment
ιατρός (ο/n)	yatros		doctor
ιδιοκτήτης/ τρια (ο/n)	eedheeokteetees/ treea		owner
ίντερνετ (το)	eenternet		internet
Ιόνιο Πέλαγος (το)	eeoneeo pelaghos		Ionian sea
ιπτάμενο δελφίνι	eeptameno dhelfeenee		hydrofoil (flying dolphin)
Ισθμός της Κορίνθου	eesthmos tees koreenthoo		Corinth Canal
ισοτιμία (n)	eesoteemeea		exchange rate

| ιστιοπλοΐα (η) | eesteeoploeea | sailing |
| ιχθυοπωλείο (το) | eekhtheeopoleeo | fishmonger's |

Κκ

κάβα (η)	kava	wine merchant, off-licence
καζίνο (το)	kazeeno	casino
καθαριστήριο (το)	kathareesteereeo	dry-cleaner's
καθαρός/ή/ό	katharos/ee/o	clean
κάθε	kathe	every, each
κάθε μέρα	kathe mera	every day
καθημερινός/ή/ό	katheemereenos/ee/o	daily
κάθισμα (το)	katheesma	seat
καθυστέρηση (η)	katheesteresee	delay
και	ke	and
καιρός (ο)	keros	weather, time

κακός/ή/ό	kakos/ee/o	bad
καλά	kala	well, all right
καλημέρα	kaleemera	good morning
καληνύχτα	kaleeneekhta	good night
καλησπέρα	kaleespera	good evening
καλοκαίρι (το)	kalokeeree	summer
καλοριφέρ (το)	kaloreefer	central heating, radiator
καλοψημένο	kalopseemeno	well done (meat)
καμπίνα (η)	kambeena	cabin
κανάλι (το)	kanalee	canal, channel (TV)
κανένας	kanenas	no-one
καντίνα (η)	kanteena	mobile roadside cafe
κάνω	kano	to do
καπέλο (το)	kapelo	hat
καπνίζω	kapneezo	to smoke
καράβι (το)	karavee	boat, ship

Greek - English

Greek - English

κάρβουνο (το)	karvoono	coal, charcoal	
στα κάρβουνα	sta karvoona	charcoal-grilled	
καρδιά (η)	kardheea	heart	
καρναβάλι (το)	karnavalee	carnival	
καροτσάκι (το)	karotsakee	pushchair	
καροτσάκι αναπηρικό	karotsakee anapeereeko	wheelchair	
κάρτα (η)	karta	card, postcard	
κάρτα	karta	boarding card	
επιβιβάσεως	epeeveevaseos		
πιστωτική κάρτα	peestoteekee karta	credit card	
κάρτοτη- λέφωνο (το)	kartoteelefono	card phone	
καρτποστάλ (το)	kartpostal	postcard	
κάστρο (το)	kastro	castle, fortress	
καταιγίδα (η)	kategheedha	storm	

καταλαβαίνω	katalaveno	to understand	
καταλαβαί-νεις; (familiar form)	katalavenees?	do you understand?	
καταλαβαί-νετε; (polite form)	katalavenete?	do you understand?	
κατάλογος (ο)	kataloghos	list, menu, directory	
κατασκήνωση (η)	kataskeenosee	camping	
κατάστημα (το)	katasteema	shop	
κατεπείγον/ κατεπείγουσα	katepeeghon/ katepeeghoosa	urgent, express	
κατηγορία (η)	kateghoreea	class (of hotel)	
κατσίκα (η)	katseeka	goat	
κάτω	kato	under, lower, down	
καύσιμα (τα)	kafseema	fuel	
καφέ	kafe	brown	

καφενείο (το)	kafeneeo	coffee house
καφές (ο)	kafes	coffee (usually Greek)
καφές γλυκός	kafes ghleekos	sweet coffee
καφές μέτριος	kafes metreeos	medium sweet coffee
καφές σκέτος	kafes sketos	strong black coffee
καφές φραπέ	kafes frape	iced coffee (Nescafé®)
καφετέρια (η)	kafetereea	cafeteria
κεντρικός/ή/ό	kendreekos/ee/o	central
κέντρο (το)	kendro	centre
κέντρο διασ-κεδάσεως	kendro dheeas-kedhaseos	nightclub
κέντρο υγείας	kendro eegheeas	health centre
κεντρικό αθλητικό κέντρο	athleeteeko kendro	sports centre
Κέρκυρα (η)	kerkeera	Corfu
κέρμα (το)	kerma	coin

κερνώ	kerno	to buy a drink
να κεράσω	na keraso	can I buy (you) a drink…?
κεφάλι (το)	kefalee	head
κεφτέδες (οι)	keftedhes	meatballs
κήπος (ο)	keepos	garden
κιβώτιο (το)	keevoteeo	large box
κιλό (το)	keelo	kilo
κίνδυνος (ο)	keendheenos	danger
κινητό (το)	keeneeto	mobile phone
κίτρινος/η/ο	keetreenos/ee/o	yellow
κλείνω	kleeno	to close
κλέφτης (ο)	kleftees	thief
κλινική (η)	kleeneekee	clinic, hospital, ward
κοιμάμαι	keemame	to sleep
κόκκινος/η/ο	kokeenos/ee/o	red
κολοκυθάκι (το)	kolokeethakee	courgette
κολύμπι (το)	koleembee	swimming

Greek – English

Greek - English

Greek		English
κολυμπώ	koleembo	to swim
κομμωτήριο (το)	komoteereeo	hairdresser's
κομπιούτερ (το)	kompyooter	computer
κοντά	konda	near
κόρη (η)	koree	daughter
κορίτσι (το)	koreetsee	young girl
κοσμήματα (τα)	kosmeemata	jewellery
κοστούμι (το)	kostoomee	man's suit
κότα (η)	kota	hen
κουβέρ (το)	koover	cover-charge
κουβέρτα (η)	kooverta	blanket, cover
κουζίνα (η)	koozeena	kitchen, cuisine
ελληνική κουζίνα	eleeneekee koozeena	Greek cuisine
κουνούπι (το)	koonoopee	mosquito
κουρείο (το)	kooreeo	barber's shop
κουτάλι (το)	kootalee	spoon
κουτί (το)	kootee	box
κρασί (το)	krasee	wine
κράτηση (η)	krateesee	reservation
κράτηση θέσης	krateese theses	seat reservation
κρέας (το)	kreas	meat
κρέας αρνίσιο	kreas arneesyo	lamb
κρέας μοσχαρίσιο	kreas moskhareesyo	beef
κρέας χοιρινό	kreas kheereeno	pork
κρεβάτι (το)	krevatee	bed
κρεβατοκάμαρα (η)	krevatokamara	bedroom
κρέμα (η)	krema	cream
κρεμμύδι (το)	kremeedhee	onion
κρεοπωλείο (το)	kreopoleeo	butcher's shop
Κρήτη (η)	kreetee	Crete
κρουαζιέρα (η)	krooazyera	cruise
κρύος/α/ο	kreeos/a/o	cold

Greek – English

Greek - English

λίτρο (το)	leetro	litre	
λογαριασμός (ο)	logharyasmos	bill	
λουκάνικο (το)	lookaneeko	sausage	
λουλούδι (το)	looloodhee	flower	
μΜ			
μαγαζί (το)	maghazee	shop	
μαγειρεύω	magheerevo	to cook	
μαγιό (το)	mayo	swimsuit	
μακαρόνια (τα)	makaronya	spaghetti, pasta	
μάλιστα	maleesta	yes, of course	
μαλλί (το)	malee	wool	
μαλλιά (τα)	malya	hair	
μάλλινος/η/ο	maleenos/ee/o	woollen	
μαμά (η)	mama	mum	
μαντήλι (το)	mandeelee	handkerchief	
μαξιλάρι (το)	makseelaree	pillow, cushion	
μαργαρίνη (η)	marghareenee	margarine	
μάρμαρο (το)	marmaro	marble	
μαρμελάδα (η)	marmeladha	jam	
μαρούλι (το)	maroolee	lettuce	
μαύρος/η/ο	mavros/ee/o	black	
μαχαίρι (το)	makheree	knife	
μαχαιροπή- ρουνα (τα)	makheroperoona	cutlery	
με	me	with	
μεγάλος/η/ο	meghalos/ee/o	large, big	
μέγαρο (το)	megharo	hall, palace, apartment block concert hall	
μέγαρο μουσικής	megharo mooseekees		
μέγεθος (το)	meghethos	size	
μέλι (το)	melee	honey	
μενού (το)	menoo	menu	
μέρα (η)	mera	day	
μερίδα (η)	mereedha	portion	
μέσα	mesa	in, inside	
μεσάνυχτα (τα)	mesaneekhta	midnight	

μεσημέρι (το)	meseemeree	midday
μεσημεριανό (το)	meseemeryano	midday meal
Μεσόγειος (η)	mesoyeeos	Mediterranean Sea
μετά	meta	after
μεταξύ	metaksee	between, among
μεταφράζω	metafrazo	to translate
μετεωρολογικό δελτίο	meteorologheeko dhelteeo	weather forecast
μετρητά (τα)	metreeta	cash
μετρό (το)	metro	underground (railway)
μηδέν	meedhen	zero
μήλο (το)	meelo	apple
μήνας (ο)	meenas	month
μήνας του μέλιτος	meenas too meleetos	honeymoon
μητέρα (η)	meetera	mother

μηχανάκι (το)	meekhanakee	moped, motorbike
μικρός/η/ό	meekros/ee/o	small
μιλάω/μιλώ	meelao/meelo	to speak
μολύβι (το)	moleevee	pencil
μόλυνση (η)	moleensee	infection, pollution
μοναστήρι (το)	monasteeree	monastery
μονόδρομος (ο)	monodhromos	one-way street
μονοπάτι (το)	monopatee	path
μόνος/η/ο	monos/ee/o	alone, only
μόνο είσοδος/ έξοδος	mono eesodhos/ eksodhos	entrance/ exit only
μοτοσυκλέτα (η)	motoseekleta	motorcycle
μουσείο (το)	mooseeo	museum
μουσική (η)	mooseekee	music
μπακάλης (ο)	bakalees	grocer
μπαμπάς (ο)	babas	dad
μπάνιο (το)	banyo	bathroom, bath

Greek - English

μπαταρία – όνομα

Greek – English

Greek	Transliteration	English
μπαταρία (η)	batareea	battery
μπιζέλια (τα)	beezelya	peas
μπισκότο (το)	beeskoto	biscuit
μπλε	ble	blue
μπλούζα (η)	blooza	jumper
μπουκάλι (το)	bookalee	bottle
μπριζόλα (η)	breezola	chop, steak
μπύρα (η)	beera	beer
Μυκήνες	meekeenes	Mycenae
μύτη (η)	meetee	nose
μωρό (το)	moro	baby
vN		
ναι	ne	yes
ναός (ο)	naos	temple, church
ναυτία (η)	nafteea	travel sickness
νεκροταφείο (το)	nekrotafeeo	cemetery
νεοελληνικά (τα)	neoeleeneeka	Modern Greek

Greek	Transliteration	English
νερό (το)	nero	water
νες, νεσκαφέ (το)	nes, neskafe	instant coffee
νεφρό (το)	nefro	kidney
νησί (το)	neesee	island
νοίκι (το)	neekee	rent
νομίζω	nomeezo	to think
νόμισμα (το)	nomeesma	coin, currency
νοσοκομείο (το)	nosokomeeo	hospital
νοσοκόμος/α (ο/η)	nosokomos/a	nurse
νότος (ο)	notos	south
νούμερο (το)	noomero	number
ντους (το)	doos	shower
νυκτερινός/ή/ό	neektereenos/ee/o	all-night (chemists, etc)
νύχτα (η)	neekhta	night

ΞΞ

ξεκουράζω	ksekoorazo	to have a rest, to relax
ξεναγός (ο/η)	ksenaghos	guide
ξενοδοχείο (το)	ksenodhokheeo	hotel
ξένος/η/ο	ksenos/ee/o	foreign
ξέρω	ksero	to know
ξεχνώ	ksekhno	to forget
ξηρός/ή/ό	kseeros/ee/o	dry
ξύλο (το)	kseelo	wood

ΟΟ

οδηγός (ο)	odheeghos	driver, guidebook
οδηγώ	odheegho	to drive
οδική βοήθεια (η)	odheekee voetheea	breakdown service
οδοντιατρείο (το)	odhondeeatreeo	dental surgery
οδοντίατρος (ο/η)	odhondeeatros	dentist
οδοντόβουρτσα (η)	odhondovoortsa	toothbrush
οδοντόκρεμα (η)	odhondokrema	toothpaste
οδός (η)	odhos	road, street
οικογένεια (η)	eekoyeneea	family
οινοπνευματώδη ποτά (τα)	eenopnevmatodhee pota	spirits
οκτώ/οχτώ	okto/okhto	eight
Ολυμπία (η)	oleempeea	Olympia
Ολυμπιακός/ή/ό	oleempeeakos/ee/o	Olympic
Όλυμπος (ο)	oleempos	Mount Olympus
όμιλος (ο)	omeelos	club
ναυτικός όμιλος	nafteekos omeelos	sailing club
ομπρέλα (η)	ombrela	umbrella
όνομα (το)	onoma	name

Greek – English

Greek – English

ονοματεπώνυμο (το)	onomateponeemo	full name
οργανωμένος/η/ο	orghanomenos/ee/o	organised
όρεξη: καλή όρεξη	kalee oreksee	enjoy your meal!
ορθόδοξος/η/ο	orthodhoksos/ee/o	orthodox
όροι ενοικιάσεως	oree eneekeeaseos	conditions of hire
ΟΣΕ	ose	Greek Railways
ΟΤΕ	ote	Greek Telecom
ούζο (το)	oozo	ouzo
όχι	okhee	no

πΠ

παϊδάκι (το)	paeedhakee	lamb chop
πάγος (ο)	paghos	ice
παίρνω	perno	to take
παγωμένος/η/ο	paghomenos/ee/o	frozen
παγωτό (το)	paghoto	ice cream
παιδικός/ή/ό	pedheekos/ee/o	for children
παιδικά σταθμός	pedeeka stathmos	children's wear crèche
πακέτο (το)	paketo	parcel, packet
Παναγία (η)	panaghea	the Virgin Mary
πανεπιστήμιο (το)	panepeesteemeeo	university
πανηγύρι (το)	panee-yeree	festival
πάντα/πάντοτε	panda/pandote	always
παντελόνι (το)	pandelonee	trousers
παντοπωλείο (το)	pandopoleeo	grocer's
παντρεμένος/η/ο	pantremenos/ee/o	married
πάνω	pano	up, on, above

Greek	Pronunciation	English
παπάς (ο)	papas	priest
πάπλωμα (το)	paploma	duvet
παππούς (ο)	papoos	grandfather
παπούτσι (το)	papootsee	shoe
παραγγέλνω	paranghelno	to order
παραγωγή: Ελληνικής παραγωγής	eleenekees paraghoghees	produce of Greece
παράθυρο (το)	paratheero	window
παρακαλώ	parakalo	please
παραλία (η)	paraleea	seashore, beach
παράσταση (η)	parastasee	performance
παρέα (η)	parea	company, group
Παρθενώνας (ο)	parthenonas	the Parthenon
πάρκο (το)	parko	park
Πάσχα (το)	paskha	Easter
πατάτα (η)	patata	potato
πατέρας (ο)	pateras	father
παυσίπονο (το)	pafseepono	painkiller
πάω	pao	to go
πεζοδρόμιο (το)	pezodhromeeo	pavement
πεθαμένος/ η/ο	pethamenos/ ee/o	dead
Πειραιάς (ο)	peereas	Piraeus
πελάτης/ πελάτισσα (ο/η)	pelatees/ pelateesa	customer
Πελοπόννησος (η)	peloponeesos	Peloponnese
περιοδικό (το)	pereeodheeko	magazine
περιοχή (η)	pereeokhee	area
περίπατος (ο)	pereepatos	walk
περίπτερο (το)	pereeptero	kiosk
πετρέλαιο (το)	petreleo	diesel fuel
πετσέτα (η)	petseta	towel

Greek – English

Greek - English

πηγαίνω	peegheno	to go
πιάτο (το)	pyato	plate, dish
πίεση αίματος	peeyesee ematos	blood pressure
πινακοθήκη (η)	peenakotheekee	art gallery
πίνω	peeno	to drink
πιπέρι (το)	peeperee	ground pepper
πιπεριά (η)	peeperya	pepper (vegetable)
πισίνα (η)	peeseena	swimming pool
πιστοποιητικό (το)	peestopyeeteeko	certificate
πιστωτική κάρτα (η)	peestoteekee karta	credit card
πίσω	peeso	behind, back
πιτζάμα (η)	peezama	pyjamas
πιτσαρία (η)	peetsareea	pizzeria
πλαζ (η)	plaz	beach
πλάι	plaee	next to
πλατεία (η)	platea	square

πληροφορίες δρομολογίων	pleeroforeeyes dhromologheeon	travel information
πληρωμή (η)	pleeromee	payment
πληρώνω	pleerono	to pay
πλοίο (το)	pleeo	ship
πλυντήριο (το)	pleenteereeo	washing machine
ποδήλατο (το)	podheelato	bicycle
ποδήλατο της θάλασσας	podheelato tees thalasas	pedalo
πόδι (το)	podhee	foot, leg
ποδόσφαιρο (το)	podhosfero	football
ποιος/ποια/ποιο	pyos/pya/pyo	who, which
ποιότητα (η)	peeoteeta	quality
πόλη (η)	polee	town, city
πολυκατάστημα (το)	poleekatasteema	department store

πολύς/πολλή/πολύ	polees/polee/polee	much, many
πονόδοντος (ο)	ponodhontos	toothache
πονοκέφαλος (ο)	ponokefalos	headache
πόνος (ο)	ponos	pain
πόρτα (η)	porta	door
πορτοκαλί (το)	portokalee	orange
πορτοφόλι (το)	portofolee	wallet
πόσα	posa	how many?
πόσο	poso	how much?
πόσο κάνει	poso kanee	how much is it?
πόσο κοστίζει	poso kosteezee	how much does it cost?
ποσότητα (η)	posoteeta	quantity
ποτάμι (το)	potamee	river
πότε;	pote?	when?
ποτέ	pote	never
ποτήρι (το)	poteeree	glass (for drinking)
ποτό (το)	poto	drink

πού;	poo?	where?
πουκάμισο (το)	pookameeso	shirt
πούλμαν (το)	poolman	coach
πουλώ	poolo	to sell
πουρμπουάρ (το)	poorbwar	tip (to waiter, etc)
πούρο (το)	pooro	cigar
πρακτορείο (το)	praktoreeo	agency
πράσινος/η/ο	praseenos/ee/o	green
πρατήριο βενζίνης	prateereeo venzeenes	petrol station
πρατήριο άρτου	prateereeo artoo	baker's
πρεσβεία (η)	presveea	embassy
πριν	preen	before
πρόεδρος (ο)	proedhros	president
προϊόν (το)	proeon	product
προκαταβολή (η)	prokatavolee	deposit

Greek - English

Greek – English

προορισμός (ο)	pro-oreesmos	destination
προπληρώνω	propleerono	to pay in advance
προσγείωση (η)	prosgheeosee	landing
προσδεθείτε	prosdhetheete	fasten safety belts
πρόσκληση (η)	proskleesee	invitation
προσοχή (η)	prosokhee	attention
πρόστιμο (το)	prosteemo	fine
πρωί η (το)	proee	morning
πρωινό (το)	proeeno	breakfast
πρωτεύουσα (η)	protevoosa	capital city
πρώτος/η/ο	protos	first
πρώτες βοήθειες	protes voeethee-es	first aid
πρώτη θέση	protee thesee	first class
πρωτοχρονιά (η)	protokhronya	New Years Day
πτήση (η)	pteesee	flight
πυροσβεστική (η)	peerosvesteekee	fire brigade
πώληση (η)	poleesee	sale
πωλητής/ήτρια(ο/η)	poletees/eetreea	sales assistant
πώς;	pos?	how?
ρΡ		
ρεζέρβα (η)	rezerva	spare wheel
ρεσεψιόν (η)	resepsyon	reception (desk)
ρέστα (τα)	resta	change (money)
ρεύμα (το)	revma	current, electricity
ρόδα (η)	rodha	wheel
ροδάκινο (το)	rodhakeeno	peach
Ρόδος (το)	rodhos	Rhodes (island)
ρολόι (το)	roloee	watch, clock
ρούχα (τα)	rookha	clothes

οςΣ

Greek	Pronunciation	English
Σαββατοκύ-ριακο (το)	savatokeeryako	weekend
σακάκι (το)	sakakee	jacket (menswear)
σαμπουάν (το)	sambooan	shampoo
σάντουιτς (το)	samdweets	sandwich
σαπούνι (το)	sapoonee	soap
σβήνω	sveno	to extinguish, to rub out
σέρβις (το)	servees	service (of car etc)
σεφ (ο)	sef	chef
σήμα (το)	seema	sign, signal
σήμερα	seemera	today
σιγά	seegha	slowly
σιδηρόδρομος (ο)	seedheerodhromos	railway
σιδηροδρομικός σταθμός (ο)	seedheerodhromeekos stathmos	railway station
σιδηροδρομι-κώς	seedheerodhromeekos	by rail
σινεμά (το)	seenema	cinema
σκάλα (η)	skala	ladder, staircase
σκηνή (η)	skeenee	tent, stage
σκι (το)	skee	ski
θαλάσσιο σκι	thalaseeo skee	water-skiing
σκόρδο (ο)	skordho	garlic
σκουπίδια (τα)	skoopeedhya	rubbish, refuse
σκυλί (το)	skeelee	dog
Σκωτία (η)	skoteea	Scotland
σκωτσέζικος/η/ο	skotsezeekos/ee/o	Scottish (thing)
Σκωτσέζος/Σκωτσέζα (ο/η)	skotsezos/skotseza	Scotsman/Scotswoman
σόμπα (η)	soba	stove, heater
σούπα (η)	soopa	soup
σπανακόπιτα (η)	spanakopeeta	spinach pie
σπίρτο (το)	speerto	match
σπίτι (το)	speetee	house, home

Greek - English

Greek	Pronunciation	English
σπιτικός/ή/ο	speeteekos/ee/o	homemade
σπορ (τα)	spor	sports
Σποράδες (οι)	sporadhes	the Sporades
στάδιο (το)	stadheeo	stadium, stage
σταθμεύω	stathmevo	to park
χώρος	khoros	parking area
σταθμεύσεως (ο)	stathmevseos	station
σιδηροδρο- μικός	seedheerodhro- meekos stathmos	railway station
σταθμός	stathmos	station
σταθμός υπεραστικών λεωφορείων	stathmos eeperas- teekon leoforeeon	bus station (intercity)
σταμάτα!	stamata!	stop!
στάση (η)	stasee	stop
στάση λεωφορείου (το)	stasee leoforeeoo	bus stop
σταυροδρόμι (το)	stavrodhromee	crossroads

Greek	Pronunciation	English
σταφύλι (το)	stafeelee	grape
στεγνοκαθα- ριστήριο (το)	steghnokatharee- steereeo	dry-cleaner's
στιγμή (η)	steeghmee	moment
συγγνώμη	seeghnomee	sorry, excuse me
συγχαρητήρια	seenkhareeteereea	congratulations
συγχωρείτε με...	me seenkhoreete	excuse me
σύζυγος (ο/η)	seezeeghos	husband/wife
συμπεριλαμ- βάνω	seempereelam- vano	to include
συμπληρώνω	seempleerono	to fill in
σύμπτωμα (το)	seemptoma	symptom
συνάλλαγμα	seenalaghma	foreign exchange
η τιμή του συναλλάγ- ματος	ee teemee too seenalalaghmatos	exchange rate
συνάντηση (η)	seenandeese	meeting

συναντώ (n)	seenando	to meet
συναυλία (η)	seenavleea	concert
συνεργείο (το)	seenergheeo	workshop, garage for car repairs
σύνορα (τα)	seenora	border, frontier
συνταγή (η)	seendaghee	prescription, recipe
συστημένη επιστολή (η)	seesteemenee epeestolee	recorded delivery
συχνά	seekhna	often
σχολείο (το)	skholeeo	school (primary)
σώμα (το)	soma	body
σωσίβιο (το)	soseeveeo	life jacket

Τ Τ

| ταβέρνα (η) | taverna | tavern with traditional food and wine |
| ταινία (η) | teneea | film, strip, tape |

ταμίας (ο/η)	tameeas	cashier
ταξί (το)	taksee	taxi
αγοραίο ταξί	aghoreo taksee	minicab (no meter)
ράδιο ταξί	radheeo taksee	radio taxi
ταξίδι (το)	takseedhee	journey, tour
καλό ταξίδι	kalo takseedhee	have a good trip
οργανωμένα ταξίδια	orghanomena takseedeea	organised tours
ταξιδιωτικό γραφείο	takseedheeoteeko ghrafeeo	travel agent
ταυτότητα (η)	taftoteeta	identity, identity card
ταχυδρομείο (το)	takheedhromeeo	post office
Ελληνικά Ταχυδρομεία (ΕΛΤΑ)	eleeneeka takheedhromeea	Greek Post Office
ταχύτητα/ταχύτης (η)	takheeteeta/takheetees	speed

Greek – English

Greek - English

τελευταίος - υπόγειος

Greek	Pronunciation	English
τελευταίος/α /ο	teleteos	last
τέλος (το)	telos	end, tax, duty
οδικά τέλη	odheeka telee	road tax
τέρμα (το)	terma	terminus, end of route
τέχνη (η)	tekhnee	art
λαϊκή τέχνη	laeekee tekhnee	folk art
τζάμι (το)	dzamee	glass (of window)
τζατζίκι (το)	tzatzeekee	tsatsiki (yoghurt, cucumber and garlic)
τηλεκάρτα (η)	teelekarta	phonecard
τηλεόραση (η)	teeleorasee	television
τηλεφώνημα (το)	teelefoneema	telephone call
τηλεφωνικός θάλαμος (ο)	teelefoneekos thalamos	phone box
τηλεφωνικός κατάλογος	teelefoneekos kataloghos	telephone directory
τηλεφωνικός κωδικός	teelefoneekos kodheekos	dialling code, area code
τι;	tee?	what?
τι είναι;	tee eenee?	what is it?
τιμή (η)	teemee	price, honour
τιμή	teemee	price of ticket, fare
εισιτηρίου	eeseeteereeoo	
τιμοκατάλογος (ο)	teemokataloghos	price list
τιμόνι (το)	teemonee	steering wheel
τίποτα	teepota	nothing
τμήμα (το)	tmeema	department, police station
το (with neuter nouns)	to	it, the
τόκος (ο)	tokos	interest (bank)
τοστ (το)	tost	toasted sandwich
τουρισμός (ο)	tooreesmos	tourism
τουρίστας/στρία (ο/η)	tooreestas/streea	tourist

Greek	Pronunciation	English
τουριστικός/ή/ό	tooreestekos/ee/o	touristic
τουριστικά είδη	tooreesteeka eedhee	souvenirs
τουριστική αστυνομία	tooreesteekee asteenomeea	Tourist Police
Τουρκία (η)	toorkea	Turkey
τραγούδι (το)	traghoodhee	song
τραγωδία (η)	traghodheea	tragedy
τράπεζα (η)	trapeza	bank
τραπεζαρία (η)	trapezarea	dining room
τραπέζι (το)	trapezee	table
τρένο (το)	treno	train
τροχαία (η)	trokhea	traffic police
τροχόσπιτο (το)	trokhospeeto	caravan, mobile home
τρώγω/τρώω	trogho/troo	to eat
τσάι (το)	tsaee	tea
τσάντα (η)	tsanda	bag
τσιγάρο (το)	tseegharo	cigarette
τυρί (το)	teeree	cheese
τυρόπιτα (η)	teeropeeta	cheese pie
τυφλός/ή/ό	teeflos/ee/o	blind
τώρα	tora	now

ΥΥ

υγεία (η)	eeyeea	health
στην υγειά σας	steen eeyeea sas	your health, cheers
υπηρεσία (η)	eepeereseea	service
ποσοστό υπηρεσίας	pososto eepeereseeas	service charge
υπόγειος/α/ο	eepoyeeos/a/o	underground
υπόγεια διάβαση πεζών	eepoyeea dheeavasee pezon	pedestrian subway
υπόγειος σι-δηρόδρομος	eepoyeeos see-dheerodhromos	underground (railway)

Greek – English

Greek - English

υπολογιστής (o)	eepologheestees	computer	
υψηλός/ή/ό	eepseelos/ee/o	high	
υψηλή τάση	eepseelee tasee	high voltage	
ύψος (το)	eepsos	height	
ύψος	eepsos	height limit	
περιορισμένο	pereeoreesmeno		

φΦ

φαγητό (το)	fayeeto	food, meal	
φαΐ (το)	faee	food	
φακός (o)	fakos	lens, torch	
φακοί επαφής	fakee epafees	contact lenses	
φακές (οι)	fakes	lentils	
φανάρι (το)	fanaree	traffic light, lantern	
φαρμακείο (το)	farmakeeo	chemist's	
φάρμακο (το)	farmako	medicine	
φάω	fao	to eat	

φεριμπότ (το)	fereebot	ferry boat	
φέτα (η)	feta	feta cheese, slice	
φιλενάδα (η)	feelenadha	girlfriend	
φιλμ (το)	feelm	film	
εμφανίσεις φιλμ	emfaneesees feelm	film developing	
φίλος/η (o/η)	feelos/ee	friend	
φίλτρο (το)	feeltro	filter	
φίλτρο λαδιού	feeltro ladheeoo	oil filter	
καφές φίλτρου	kafes feeltroo	filter coffee	
φλας (το)	flas	flash (camera), indicators (on car)	
φοιτητής/ φοιτήτρια (o/η)	feeteetees/ feeteetreea	student	
φοιτητικό εισιτήριο (το)	feeteeteeko eeseeteereeo	student fare	
φόρεμα (το)	forema	dress	
φόρος (o)	foros	tax	

φούρνος (ο)	foornos	oven, bakery
ΦΠΑ (ο)	feepea	VAT
φρένο (το)	freno	brake (in car)
φρέσκος/ια/ο	freskos/ya/o	fresh
φρούτο (το)	frooto	fruit
φύλακας (ο)	feelakas	guard
φύλαξη αποσκευών (η)	feelaksee aposkevon	left-luggage office
φως (το)	fos	light
φωτιά (η)	fotya	fire
φωτογραφία (η)	fotoghrafeea	photograph
φωτογραφίζω	fotoghrafeezo	to take photographs
μη φωτογραφίζετε	me fotoghrafeezete	no photographs
φωτογραφική μηχανή (η)	fotoghrafeekee mekhanee	camera
φωτοτυπία (η)	fototeepeea	photocopy

Χ χ

χαίρετε	kherete	hello (polite)
χάπι (το)	khapee	pill
χάρτης (ο)	khartees	map
οδικός χάρτης	odheekos khartees	road map
χαρτί (το)	khartee	paper
χαρτί κουζίνας	khartee koozeenas	kitchen paper
χαρτομάντηλο (το)	khartomandeelo	tissue
χαρτονόμισμα (το)	khartonomeesma	banknote
χειροποίητος/η/ο	kheeropee-eetos/ee/o	handmade
χειροτεχνία (η)	kheerotekhneea	handicraft
χειρούργος (ο)	kheeroorghos	surgeon
χέρι (το)	kheree	hand, arm
χιλιόμετρο (το)	kheelyometro	kilometre
χιόνι (το)	khyonee	snow
χορός (ο)	khoros	dance

Greek - English

χορτοφάγος (ο/η)	khortofaghos	vegetarian
χρειάζομαι	khreeazome	to need
χρήματα (τα)	khreemata	money
χρηματοκι-βώτιο (το)	khreematokeevo-teeo	safe (for valuables)
χρήση (η)	khreesee	use
οδηγίες χρήσεος	odheegheees khreeseos	instructions for use
χρήσιμος/η/ο	khreeseemos/ee/o	useful
χρησιμοποιώ	khreeseemopeeo	to use
Χριστιανός/ή	khreesteeanos/ee	Christian
Χριστούγεννα (το)	khreestoogena	Christmas
Καλά Χρι-στούγεννα	kala khreestooyena	Merry Christmas
χρόνος (ο)	khronos	time, year
χρυσός/ή/ό	khreesos/ee/o	(made of) gold
χρώμα (το)	khroma	colour, paint
χτες	khtes	yesterday

χυμός (ο)	kheemos	juice
χώρα (η)	khora	country
χωριάτικο ψωμί (το)	khoryateeko psomee	bread (round, flat loaf)
χωριό (το)	khoreeo	village
χωρίς	khorees	without
χώρος (ο)	khoros	area, site
αρχαιολογικός χώρος	arkheologheekos khoros	archaeological site
ιδιωτικός χώρος	eedheeoteekos khoros	private land
χώρος σταθμεύσεως	khoros stathmefseos	parking area

ψ Ψ

ψάρεμα (το)	psarema	fishing
ψαρεύω	psarevo	to fish
ψάρι (το)	psaree	fish
ψαρόβαρκα (η)	psarovarka	fishing boat

ψαροταβέρνα (η)	psarotaverna	fish tavern
ψητός/ή/ό	pseetos/ee/o	roasted, grilled
ψυγείο (το)	pseegheeo	fridge, radiator (of car)
ψωμί (το)	psomee	bread

ωΩ

ωτοστόπ (το)	otostop	hitchhiking
ώρα (η)	ora	time, hour
ώρες	ores	visiting hours
επισκέψεως	epeeskepseos	
ώρες	ores	opening hours
λειτουργίας	leetoorgheeas	
της ώρας	tees oras	freshly cooked (food)
ωραίος/α/ο	oreos/a/o	beautiful, nice
ωράριο (το)	orareeo	timetable
ως	os	as, while

Greek – English

Further titles in Collins' phrasebook range
Collins Gem Phrasebook

Also available as **Phrasebook CD Pack**
Other titles in the series

Arabic	Greek	Polish
Cantonese	Italian	Portuguese
Croatian	Japanese	Russian
Czech	Korean	Spanish
Dutch	Latin American	Thai
French	Spanish	Turkish
German	Mandarin	Vietnamese

Collins Phrasebook & Dictionary

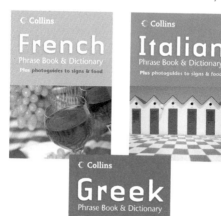

Also available as **Phrasebook CD Pack**
Other titles in the series
German Japanese Portuguese Spanish

Collins Easy: Photo Phrasebook

Also available as
**Phrasebook
CD Pack**

**Other titles
in the series**
Easy French
Easy Greek
Easy Italian

To order any of these titles, please telephone
0870 787 1732. For further information about all
Collins books, visit our website: www.collins.co.uk